CULTIVATE AND KEEP

An Economic Foundation for the Great Restoration

Doug Tjaden

Copyright © 2023 by Douglas Tjaden

All rights reserved.

ISBN 978-1-7357090-6-2

Except where indicated, Scripture quotations are taken from the New American Standard Bible® (NASB), Copyright © 1960, 1962, 1963, 1968, 1971, 1972, 1973, 1975, 1977, 1995 by The Lockman Foundation.

Used by permission. www.Lockman.org

Scripture quotations are taken from the New King James Version®. Copyright © 1982 by Thomas Nelson.

Used by permission. All rights reserved.

This publication may not be reproduced, stored in a retrieval system with public access, or transmitted in any form or by any means—electronic, mechanical, photocopy, recording, or otherwise—without permission of the author.

Printed in the United States of America

First Edition Released September 10, 2023
Revised January 2026

"Then the LORD God took the man and put him into the garden of Eden to cultivate it and keep it."

- God soon after creation

"The garden is now larger, as are the blessings of honoring My covenant with you."

- God today.

Table of Contents

Foreword i

Introduction v

Part 1 The First Covenant

Chapter 1 Our Relationship with Creation 1

Chapter 2 The Covenant 7

Chapter 3 The Covenant Broken 15

Chapter 4 The Cost 25

Part 2 Understanding the Times

Chapter 5 Reality Check 35

Chapter 6 Monetary Reality 43

Chapter 7 Economic Reality 51

Chapter 8 Food Reality 61

Part 3 Covenant Restored

Chapter 9 Apply a New Economic Worldview 71

Chapter 10 Know Your Trading Floors 87

Chapter 11 Redeem the Land 99

Chapter 12 An Invitation 111

Acknowledgments 117

Foreword

By Joel Salatin

"God's in control." "God's got this." Every time I'm in a church setting and hear Christians cavalierly invoke these assumptions I want to counter "Oh really?" It's true God *can* do anything, but He often doesn't. Instead, *He expects us to do what we know is right.*

Unfortunately, we often don't. Thus, His "plan B" jumps off the Bible's pages. Adam and Eve eating the forbidden fruit was plan B. The flood was plan B. Aaron as Moses' spokesman was plan B. While God's sovereignty and power find expression in taking plan B and still orchestrating His ultimate redemptive plan, how much better would it be if we adhered to "plan A?"

What if instead of asking God to heal us after a life of couch potatoing and Doritos we honored His design for our bodies, using them and fueling them the way He intended? What if instead of filling prayer requests with healing children's physical and emotional dysfunction, we quit dosing them with ultra-processed fish crackers and sugar pops in the church nursery?

On a macro cultural scale, the American faith community too often abdicates its call to be salt and light and challenge the kings of the earth. The divorce rate and sickness rate, to name just two dysfunctions, are no different in the faith community than among nonbelievers. Why? One reason is that in a western linear compartmentalized segregated mentality, many Americans adhere to the Augustinian notion that spiritual and physical occupy two different worlds. That God isn't all that interested in physical; He cares only about the spiritual. Everything else is negotiable.

A second reason is the notion that our communities and culture sinking into debauchery and dysfunction is to be expected since Satan rules the earth and God is going to zap us out before things get really dicey during the tribulation. Reality is, the Bible shows us God has always used difficult times and persecution to purify His people.

So, what are we Christians supposed to do today? In this short but fabulous little book, Doug Tjaden walks us through the imperatives for working out our faith in this physical world as prologue to the spiritual. It begins with God's original covenant with Adam and Eve to steward Creation *properly* for the benefit of all humanity. It connects the godlessness of Noah's day to the identical thinking that led to contrivances of modern banking and capitalism. Oh, did I dare to impugn capitalism?

Try this sentence on for size: "As difficult as it may be for many to accept, competition and ownership, as understood and practiced by many, if not most, followers of Jesus, are the leaven in capitalism." These and many other observations in this book challenge the assumptions of the conservative faith community. Doug's thesis (in my words) is that worldview capture of the Christian community has emasculated both our influence and our ability to live according to God's plan A.

The Christian's identity and responsibility are far more than reciting the Apostle's creed. When advocating for compost over chemicals or authentic food over ultra processed, I often use the simple question "Does God care?" If God cares about the sparrow that falls and the number of hairs on our head, surely He cares about everything from the "creeping things" He created to nurture our soil, to what kind of businesses we fund with our disposable income.

Assuming God sits in the heavens simply listening for our verbal assent to Christ's atonement and that's all that matters, is a shallow and incomplete understanding of being created "in the image of God." As an economist, Doug dares to challenge us with a broad view of "trading floors." He points out that even our conversations are trading floors where value is created and exchanged. Succinct and precise, this little book compresses profound Biblical insight into hard-hitting daily decision-making and practice.

I've often thought about the intellectual and spiritual schizophrenia exhibited by folks sitting in the pew advocating the Golden Rule (do unto others as you would have them do unto you) and then serving Tyson factory chicken in the after-service potluck. Factory grown chicken dishonors the life of the chicken, stinks up the neighborhood with fecal particulate, and fills humans with toxicity, pathogens, and nutrient deficiency. How's that for loving your neighbor?

Doug is a kindred spirit, daring to challenge the largely world-compliant faith community with a new responsibility to truly act out our beliefs in a visible, tangible way. Whether we buy a car from this outfit or that matters. Whether we fill our plate with this food or that matters. In a time when defunding is in vogue, it's time for the Christian community to quit playing footsies with the "kings of the earth" and start representing the interests of the King of Kings and Lord of Lords. Such living requires each of us who name the name of Christ to get visceral and practical about the physical manifestations of our faith at a fundamental level.

Cultivate and Keep is a must-read primer for believers who desire to match talk and walk. After all, the commendation we aspire to hear is not "well believed, thou good and faithful servant," but "well DONE, thou good and faithful servant." This book makes clear the difference.

Joel Salatin, Polyface Farms
Editor, The Stockman Grassfarmer

Introduction

Over the next decade, the design of every system that manages interactions between human beings is going to change dramatically. The worldview of those who design these systems will determine the quality of life for every human on the planet for generations. None of these systems are more important than those that manage the storage and deployment of the value we create through the fruit of our labor.

Unfortunately, few people are interested in discussing this thing we call "economics." They have bad memories of sitting in their high school or college economic classes listening to instructors drone on in a monotone voice about charts and graphs and curves. This wouldn't be a problem if our present systems were designed and operated according to biblical principles.

However, they are so anti-biblical that they do immeasurable harm to humanity in general and the body of Christ in particular. One reason this harm is so great is because *economics is ubiquitous. This means it touches the lives of every human being, every day of their lives.* Yet, because it has been framed as boring and beyond the intellectual understanding of most people, few followers of Jesus stop to consider that God might expect His children to be directly involved in creating and managing economic systems. After all, they direct the flow of value created by those who bear His image for a specific purpose – to build His Kingdom. Instead, His children are content to embrace systems designed to benefit the kings of the earth.

How did we become so apathetic?

The answer is stunningly, frustratingly, simple. Francis Chan identifies it in his book *Letters to the Church.*

"Many of us have become so accustomed to *various traditions* that we genuinely think they are commanded [in Scripture]. I have seen people become furious over the absence of Sunday school while being indifferent toward the absence of the Lord's Supper. Some rant over the style of music while shrugging their shoulders at the neglect of widows and orphans in their distress. It may surprise some of you that a forty-minute sermon isn't commanded but "bear one another's burdens, and so fulfill the law of Christ" is actually in the Bible."[1] (emphasis mine)

Various traditions.

The body of Christ today has little understanding of the enormous damage the "traditions of men" cause to God's Kingdom. They quite literally make "the Word of God of no effect"[2] in our lives. The following statement is the first of several that you may find controversial in this book.

Of all the traditions of men that today nullify the Word of God on earth, none have caused more damage to humanity throughout history than those embedded in the economic and monetary systems of the world.

It is a historically and biblically proven reality that God's people have embraced systems designed by the kings of the earth that are among the grossest abominations the world has ever encountered. They have left billions of human beings in despair, while simultaneously decimating God's Creation. Yet, today, the church has a stunning lack of awareness of this reality, let alone an understanding of how we became economic slaves to such systems.

When I began writing this book, I knew God had something specific in mind, although I was not exactly sure how He wanted me to communicate it. What emerged over the next several months was a multi-layered story that includes worldview, economic principles, Creation, food, and how critical it is to understand how intertwined they are in today's rapidly changing world.

And that leads me to the dual purpose of writing this book. The first reason is simple. Followers of Jesus should naturally want to adopt an economic system based on God's principles and ways. Yet, since most have been lulled to sleep by the economic traditions of men, that reason is not enough to cause us to take action. The second reason is a bit more ominous. Twenty-five years ago, William Strauss and

---
[1] Francis Chan, *Letters to the Church*, pg 48
[2] Mark 7:13 NKJV

Neil Howe released a book entitled *The Fourth Turning*. I read this book in the early 2000s and have since watched their predictions unfold with uncanny accuracy.

Strauss and Howe reveal four cycles, or "turnings," that occur as specific types of generations shape the culture, economy, and political landscape. Over the last few hundred years, in particular, these turnings have become relatively predictable in timing and sequence. The complete cycle takes about eighty years. For context, the three previous "fourth turnings" occurred roughly during the years 1770-1790, 1850-1870, and 1930-1950. If you know your history, you know what occurred during each of those time periods – the Revolutionary War, the Civil War, and the Great Depression and World War II.

That fact alone should grab our attention and cause us to at least have some level of concern about what is happening in the world today. In fact, in early 2023, Neil Howe released a sequel to his 1999 work entitled *The Fourth Turning is Here*.[3] He makes the case that we are in a fourth turning that began around 2010 in the wake of the Great Recession. If that is true (and evidence is overwhelming that it is), it means we are well into the second half of this fourth turning. This period has historically been marked by substantial and increasing levels of turmoil. This is precisely what we see in the year 2025.

My friends, the world faces major challenges. Sadly, much of the modern Western church is not equipped to deal with them. A study by the Cultural Research Center at Arizona Christian University released in May of 2022 revealed that only 37% of pastors and 12% of youth pastors in the United States hold a biblical worldview.[4] Those numbers are stunning. Yet they only measure a *general* biblical worldview. With our ignorance of economics, what percentage of church leaders do you think embrace a biblical *economic* worldview?

As we move toward the conclusion of the present fourth turning, to say that this is concerning is a gross understatement. If the church continues to embrace a secular economic worldview, complete with its Word-nullifying traditions, at the end of this fourth turning the kings

---

[3] https://www.amazon.com/s?k=the+fourth+turning+is+here+paperback
[4] https://www.arizonachristian.edu/2022/05/12/shocking-lack-of-biblical-worldview-among-american-pastors/

of the earth will create a world of economic tyranny and hardship that is historic in its scope.

Before you get depressed and stop reading, let me assure you, God is on the move. For the first time in history, the church can unite worldwide and navigate these massive changes, *if* we fix our eyes on *God* and what *He* is doing. As I see it, He has something very different in mind—a period when followers of Jesus initiate a "Great Restoration" of His principles and ways.

This requires followers of Jesus to speak "economic truth" and no longer fear offending the citizens of Babylon—or fellow followers of Jesus who have found refuge in its economic and monetary traditions. We must propose new solutions to our economic and monetary problems that are thoroughly grounded in God's "radical" ways.

To do this we must have the courage to open God's Word and let it take us where it will. If we do, an incredible story awaits us. One that begins where you would expect. "In the beginning." It is a story of God's love for humanity, Creation, His Son, and the incredible relationship He intended us to all enjoy, which, by-the-way, was designed to protect humanity from the very threats we face today.

During this time of uncertainty and rapid change, we can build systems based on God's principles that will produce what is necessary to live the life of abundance that Jesus came to give.[5] As in the past, today God is drawing together a remnant who is willing to embrace His "radical" ways, regardless of the cost. The prototypes we build together will become the economic and monetary systems upon which communities and nations will thrive in the coming years.

Note: While this book introduces substantial new material, it leans heavily on the concepts and biblical support in *I Came to Give* and *My Ways*. These two books provide a helpful reference and connect important principles in this book to our present reality. As such, you will find key excerpts included in this book.

---

[5] John 10:10

Part 1
The First Covenant

Chapter 1
Our Relationship with Creation

> "All things came into being through Him, and apart from Him nothing came into being that has come into being."
> John 1:3

Stories both describe and change the world. It has always been that way. The Bible is a series of stories about people and supernatural entities as they interact with God, His Son, His Creation, and other human beings. Scripture is ultimately a story about how God intended these relationships to work together so that His Kingdom would be spread across the entire earth.[6]

For the first forty years of my life, I did not appreciate the gift God had given me in my youth to witness these relationships in action while growing up on a small wheat farm in rural southwest Nebraska. Looking back, I now have a deep appreciation for the relationships we developed with the co-stewards of Creation in our little town. That, along with my love for running our combine and watching a year's worth of hard work get gobbled up and tucked away in the bin behind me, was the reason I intended to stay on the farm. God, however, had other plans.

Unfortunately, the 1970s was a decade marked by high inflation. Making a living on the farm was difficult. The economic hardship took a toll on my father. He did not see a practical path to transferring our small farm to me and my future family. Instead, he felt that a college education would provide me with a path to a better life.

So, in 1980, I headed off to Kearney State College in central Nebraska. Sadly, my departure from our family farm was part of a

---
[6] Matthew 6:10

growing trend. Over the following decades, countless heirs of family farms walked away from the privilege of interacting with and stewarding Creation to pursue "the American Dream." This was never God's intention.

Nurturing the ground, planting seeds, and watching them produce abundant life-sustaining food is nothing short of a miracle. From the beginning of time, God intended that cultivating and keeping Creation would be a primary centering point for every human being to relate to Him, His Son, Creation itself, and our neighbors.

In fact, providing life-giving sustenance to our fellow human beings was meant to be one of the most honored positions anyone could hold in His Kingdom. Support for this rather bold assertion is easy to see when we start…

In the Beginning

Most people default to Genesis 1:1 as the starting point of the biblical narrative. While technically not accurate, it generally causes no harm when developing biblical doctrine. That is not the case for us. To set the proper biblical context for what you are about to read, the correct chronological starting point is critical. And that starting point is the book of John.

> "In the beginning was the Word, and the Word was with God, and the Word was God. He was in the beginning with God. All things came into being through Him, and apart from Him nothing came into being that has come into being. In Him was life, and the life was the Light of men. The Light shines in the darkness, and the darkness did not comprehend it."
> John 1:1-5

These few verses set important context for understanding the Creation narrative in Genesis 1 and 2. They also help us interpret other New Testament passages that reveal the critical role Jesus plays in the biblical story prior to His coming to earth. Let's look at two of them.

> "[Jesus] is the image of the invisible God, the firstborn of all creation. For by Him all things were created, both in the heavens and on earth, visible and invisible, whether thrones or dominions or rulers or authorities—all things have been

Chapter 1: Our Relationship with Creation

created through Him and for Him. He is before all things, and in Him all things hold together."
Colossians 1:15-17

"God, after He spoke long ago to the fathers in the prophets in many portions and in many ways, in these last days has spoken to us in His Son, whom He appointed heir of all things, through whom also He made the world. And He is the radiance of His glory and the exact representation of His nature, and upholds all things by the word of His power."
Hebrews 1:1-3a

Building on John 1:1-5 and examining the Greek definition of several key words and phrases opens the door to a wonderful discovery. In all three passages, the word "through" in Greek is *dia*, which means "the channel of an act; because of; by occasion of, by reason of, for the sake of." In Colossians 1:17, the Greek word for "hold together" is *synistaō*, and it means "to place together, to set in the same place, to bring or band together." Finally, in Hebrews 1:3, the Greek words for "upholds," "all things," "word," and "power" are *pherō, pas, rhēma, and dynamos*. They mean to bring forward and bear up everything through the power residing in a thing by virtue of its nature, using a spoken word.

There is a lot packed in here that is easily overlooked on a casual reading. However, these verses form the foundation of an exciting narrative about the fullness of what occurred during the act of creation. Combined, they tell us that...

Through the spoken Word of the Father, Creation came into existence for the sake of the Son. It is held together physically and remains in existence today by virtue of who Jesus is and by the power of His Word.

Please read that again. The implications are stunning. Here we have irrefutable evidence that the Father, Son, and Creation are intimately intertwined with one another, and that without Jesus "nothing came into being that has come into being." Without the presence and power of Jesus, Creation would cease to exist. This gives us a much fuller context to understand the statement:

Jesus is God's *entire* provision for us.

There is not a faithful Bible teacher, pastor, or follower of Jesus who would not agree that Jesus is God's "entire provision" to attain eternal spiritual life. However, we now know that the physical universe also is sustained by, through, and for Jesus. That includes your body and mine. It includes every plant and animal on earth that God gave us for food.[7] In every way imaginable, we depend on Jesus to sustain both our spiritual *and* physical lives. Now consider the following verse with that in mind.

> "And my God will supply *all your needs* according to His riches in glory in Christ Jesus."
> Philippians 4:19 (emphasis mine)

In this passage, the Greek word for "in" is *en* and it means "a fixed position in place, time, or state." This reinforces the idea that *all* our needs, including the sustenance needed from Creation to keep us physically alive, are quite literally found "in" Jesus. From the beginning, God planned for Jesus to be the source of the physical life our bodies receive through Creation *and* the spiritual life we receive as members of God's Kingdom. This reality sheds new light and expands the contextual meaning of passages such as the following.

> "Jesus then said to them, "Truly, truly, I say to you, it is not Moses who has given you the bread out of heaven, but it is My Father who gives you the true bread out of heaven. For the bread of God is that which comes down out of heaven, and gives life to the world." Then they said to Him, "Lord, always give us this bread." Jesus said to them, "I am the bread of life; he who comes to Me will not hunger, and he who believes in Me will never thirst."
> John 6:32-35

> "Believe Me that I am *in* the Father and the Father is *in* Me;"
> John 14:11a (emphasis mine)

---

[7] Genesis 1:29

Chapter 1: Our Relationship with Creation

"Abide *in* Me, and I *in* you. As the branch cannot bear fruit of itself unless it abides *in* the vine, so neither can you unless you abide *in* Me. I am the vine, you are the branches; he who abides *in* Me and I *in* him, he bears much fruit, *for apart from Me you can do nothing.*"
John 15:4-5 (emphasis mine)

"For our citizenship is in heaven, from which also we eagerly wait for a Savior, the Lord Jesus Christ; who will transform the body of our humble state into conformity with the body of His glory, *by the exertion of the power that He has even to subject all things to Himself.*"
Philippians 3:20-21 (emphasis mine)

Now, consider this expanded context to the following passages:

"We have seen and testify that the Father has sent the Son to be the Savior *of the world.*"
1 John 4:14 (emphasis mine)

"The next day he saw Jesus coming to him and said, 'Behold, the Lamb of God who takes away the sin *of the world!*'"
John 1:29 (emphasis mine)

We have been taught that these verses, and others like them, mean that Jesus takes away the sin of all the *people* on earth. However, the Greek word for "world" used in these verses is *kosmos*, which means "orderly arrangement, i.e., decoration; by implication, the world in a wide or narrow sense, *including [but not exclusively]* its inhabitants."

Maybe, just as in Philippians 4:19, where "all" means "all," in these verses "the world" means *the entire earth,* as well as its inhabitants. This more literal view makes sense when considering passages such as the following.

"For the anxious longing of the creation waits eagerly for the revealing of the sons of God. For the creation was subjected to futility, not willingly, but because of Him who subjected it, in hope that the creation itself also will be set free from its slavery to corruption into the freedom of the glory of the

children of God. For we know that the whole creation groans and suffers the pains of childbirth together until now."
Romans 8:19-22

As I read these verses, I can now better empathize with how the Father and Son must feel as they watch Creation groan and suffer under humanity's mismanagement, in large part due to our ignorance of its intimate relationship with Jesus and its valued place in God's original plan. Now let me be clear. I am not saying that all of Creation is alive in the literal sense of that word. I am saying what Scripture says. God, Jesus, and Creation have a deep relationship with one another that we cannot fully understand.

As we continue to examine the Creation narrative, we will see that God entrusted humanity with the responsibility to properly steward this incredible gift. Understanding the critical nature of this responsibility hinges on the proper chronological sequencing of John 1:1-5, Genesis 2:15, and Genesis 1:28. In other words, we must get the beginning of the story right.

Chapter 2
The Covenant

"Then the LORD God took the man and put him into the garden of Eden to cultivate it and keep it."
Genesis 2:15

God always has a reason for what He does and when He does it. By beginning our examination of the creation narrative in John 1:1-5, we discovered that humanity has a special and intimate relationship with God the Father and Creation through Jesus. Since God is about relationships, it should come as no surprise that the Creation narrative would reveal an economic system that is designed to build His Kingdom based on *relationships* and not *transactions*.

In doing so, God provided humanity with a system capable of managing vast resources that would bless all generations. Therefore, we should expect that the Creation narrative will also reveal to us the foundational principles upon which this system must be managed throughout time. And indeed, it does.

It begins with the first two days of Creation as God brought the heavens and the earth into existence and separated the waters between them. By the end of day two, God had established the foundational building blocks—land and water—from which all resources required to build His Kingdom would be produced. Then came day three.

"Then God said, 'Let the earth sprout vegetation, plants yielding seed, and fruit trees on the earth bearing fruit after their kind with seed in them'; and it was so. The earth brought forth vegetation, plants yielding seed after their kind, and trees bearing fruit with seed in them, after their kind; and God saw

that it was good. There was evening and there was morning, a
third day."
Genesis 1:11-13

You have probably read these verses countless times. Yet it is easy to overlook the single word that identifies the core design element that enables Creation to provide humanity with the resources necessary to fulfill its purpose.

Seed.

Because of seed, every plant, animal, sea creature, creeping thing, and yes, human, can reproduce. Not just once, but forever. We are only halfway through the first chapter of the Bible and God has revealed the cornerstone (seed) of the foundation (land and water) that will generate, *in perpetuity*, the resources necessary for humanity to spread His Kingdom throughout the earth. And please do not lose sight of the fact that the power to uphold this system comes through our Lord, Savior, and King - Jesus.

As we continue, take a moment and reflect on what is unfolding here. Already, it is hard to comprehend the genius of God's design. Yet He is just getting started!

"God made the two great lights, the greater light to govern
the day, and the lesser light to govern the night; He made
the stars also. God placed them in the expanse of the
heavens to give light on the earth, and to govern the day
and the night, and to separate the light from the darkness;
and God saw that it was good. There was evening and
there was morning, a fourth day."
Genesis 1:16-19

On day four, God created a critical component to sustain this new ecosystem. He put the sun in place to activate the process of photosynthesis, which is necessary for plants to grow and reproduce. He placed the moon to govern the cycle of tides, which circulate the ocean waters, so they do not stagnate, and thus, can support life. This "water cycle" moves life-giving water into the sky, where it is carried to the ends of the earth. By the end of day four, God had created a

Chapter 2: The Covenant

natural hydration system for both plants and land animals. Pretty awesome in my view!

> "Then God said, "Let the waters teem with swarms of living creatures, and let birds fly above the earth in the open expanse of the heavens." God created the great sea monsters and every living creature that moves, with which the waters swarmed after their kind, and every winged bird after its kind; and God saw that it was good. There was evening and there was morning, a fifth day."
> Genesis 1:20-21,23

On day five, God revealed another key design principle of His Creation. Abundance. This is one of the first clues of the depth of His love for humanity and Creation. The desire of His heart, as expressed by the Son who upholds it in John 10:10, is that we may have life and have it abundantly![8]

> "Then God said, "Let the earth bring forth living creatures after their kind: cattle and creeping things and beasts of the earth after their kind"; and it was so. God made the beasts of the earth after their kind, and the cattle after their kind, and everything that creeps on the ground after its kind; and God saw that it was good."
> Genesis 1:24-25

God could have been satisfied with a world where land and water produced vegetation that would sustain humanity throughout time. However, God is not about doing just what is necessary. He chose to provide a diversity of life for us to enjoy because He loves His people, His Son, and His Creation. He wants us to enjoy a life of rich diversity in relationships that we can only experience through a life of abundance and a sense of awe and wonder at the love of our Creator!

> "Then God said, 'Let Us make man in Our image, according to Our likeness;"
> Genesis 1:26a

---

[8] John 10:10

This is where the Creation narrative begins to reveal why proper stewardship of Creation is critical in God's grand plan to build His Kingdom on earth. To understand the chronology correctly, we must pause at Genesis 1:26a and turn to Genesis 2:7.

> "Then the LORD God formed man of dust from the ground, and breathed into his nostrils the breath of life; and man became a living being."

Note that God did not create man *ex-nihilo*—that is, out of nothing. The text tells us He created man from the established elements already placed into Creation. This supports the assertion made in the previous chapter about the nature of the relationships God intends us to have. The Father (the breath of life), the earthly, natural world (Creation), and the Son (through whom it occurs and is held together by the power of His Word) all participate in the creation of humans.

The relevant verses that chronologically precede and follow this act identify a critical God-given responsibility that humans were given as participants in this relational bond. The first identifies a problem.

> "Now no shrub of the field was yet in the earth, and no plant of the field had yet sprouted, for the LORD God had not sent rain upon the earth, and there was no man to cultivate the ground."
> Genesis 2:5

The second identifies the solution to the problem.

> "Then the LORD God took the man and put him into the garden of Eden to cultivate it and keep it."
> Genesis 2:15

These two verses explicitly reveal humanity's primary responsibility in our relationship with Creation. To fully understand it requires examining the Hebrew text.

The word for "cultivate" is *ābar*. It is used 290 times in Scripture, and its primary root means "to serve." It is also used several times in the context of "worshipper." The Hebrew word for "keep" is *šâmar*, meaning to "guard, observe, give heed, have charge of, keep watch and ward, protect, save life."

Creation needed stewards to serve it, or in other words, to manage it so that it could sustainably produce in amazing abundance. That part seems logical. However, this directive was given before the Fall. Why did God also say Adam needed to "protect it?" In a sinless world, what would it need to be protected from? In hindsight, it seems obvious. God knew the plans of the one who would soon seek to steal, kill, and destroy all that God had created. Therefore, God's directive came with a specific command that contained an important restriction.

> "The LORD God commanded the man, saying, "From any tree of the garden you may eat freely; but from the tree of the knowledge of good and evil you shall not eat, for in the day that you eat from it you will surely die."
> Genesis 2:16-17

God was very clear. Of all My Creation, pay particular attention to "keeping" this tree. Do not come near it. Do not let any other entity come near it. If you fail, it will unleash consequences beyond what you can imagine. With His warning given, God provided Creation with the final, beautiful piece that enabled humanity to fulfill its intended purpose.

> "Then the LORD God said, "It is not good for the man to be alone; I will make him a helper suitable for him… So the LORD God caused a deep sleep to fall upon the man, and he slept; then He took one of his ribs and closed up the flesh at that place. The LORD God fashioned into a woman the rib which He had taken from the man, and brought her to the man."
> Genesis 2:18,21-22

When God created Eve by taking her out of Adam's body, it further demonstrated His commitment to connect man, woman, Creation, and Jesus with Himself in the most intimate possible way physically and spiritually. Doing so made her fully "suitable" to become a "helper" just as the Hebrew word describes—part opposite; specifically a counterpart, or mate. Only after creating woman did

God declare His Creation was "very good." It was finished. There was nothing more to add. He had established a human family. Through His Son, and the Creation He upholds, this family had everything they needed to accomplish His purpose, which brings us now to Genesis 1:28.

> "God blessed them; and God said to them, 'Be fruitful and multiply, and fill the earth, and subdue it; and rule over the fish of the sea and over the birds of the sky and over every living thing that moves on the earth.' Then God said, 'Behold, I have given you every plant yielding seed that is on the surface of all the earth, and every tree which has fruit yielding seed; it shall be food for you; and to every beast of the earth and to every bird of the sky and to every thing that moves on the earth which has life, I have given every green plant for food'; and it was so. God saw all that He had made, and behold, it was very good. And there was evening and there was morning, the sixth day. Thus the heavens and the earth were completed, and all their hosts. By the seventh day God completed His work which He had done, and He rested on the seventh day from all His work which He had done. Then God blessed the seventh day and sanctified it, because in it He rested from all His work which God had created and made."
> Genesis 1:28-2:3

To ensure humanity could walk in the fullness of this blessing, God created a universe in which He strategically initiated intimate relationships between Himself, His Son, Creation, and humans. Each became a party to a de facto covenant with one another to establish a global Kingdom on earth.

The word "covenant" is used here very purposefully. It is a serious claim with major implications for honoring the responsibilities we have with the relationships previously described. Therefore, let me take a moment and establish what qualifies it as a covenant.

Bible scholars generally agree that there is a "covenantal framework" in Scripture that contains covenants both declared and undeclared by God. Those that are undeclared contain several key characteristics.

Chapter 2: The Covenant

1. *Covenantal Connection*: The actions in the undeclared covenant are intimately linked with other covenants. For example, the Feast of Unleavened Bread is not directly named by God as a covenant. However, it is directly linked to the Passover. The Passover is a key moment in God's covenant with Abraham and his descendants, marking their deliverance and their subsequent covenantal commitment to God. It should not escape our notice that there is a direct link between growing, harvesting, preparing, and consuming food and these early covenants.

2. *Permanent Ordinance*: The Feast of Unleavened Bread is commanded as a permanent ordinance, to be observed from generation to generation. This perpetual nature aligns with the concept of covenant, which involves ongoing obligations and memorials. The first two chapters have sufficiently established the perpetual need for humanity to be in intimate relationship with God and His Son by serving and protecting Creation.

3. *Covenantal Obedience*: Upholding or failing to uphold a covenant has serious consequences that reach throughout the generations. God's people must cultivate and keep Creation if they are to walk in His blessing and to "be fruitful and multiply and subdue (establish His Kingdom throughout) the earth."

4. *Symbolic Significance*: Upholding the terms of the covenant becomes a symbol in other teachings. Growing and consuming food plays a central role throughout Scripture, especially in Jesus' life and teachings. The last relational gathering of Jesus and His disciples before His death gave birth to the permanent ordinance practiced today as the sacrament of communion.

A more familiar example of a covenant that we all recognize, but is not named specifically in Scripture, is marriage. We refer to it as a covenant, because the defining characteristics of a covenant are inherently present in this relationship between a man and woman.

Similarly, these characteristics are plainly evident in the relationships God established between Himself, Creation, and humanity during the Creation narrative. The intimate and perpetual nature of these relationships, along with the requirement that each party fulfill specific responsibilities for the covenant to be enforceable, supports a covenantal view. Finally, covenants must produce a specific outcome that will benefit each of its participants:

1. *God* provides an incredible, diverse natural ecosystem for humanity.
2. *His Son* upholds and sustains this ecosystem by the power of His word.
3. *Humanity* is to cultivate and keep the ecosystem—to serve and protect it.
4. *Creation* will "give up its strength"[9] to yield an abundance of the human and natural resources necessary to build the Kingdom of God on earth.

All of this was God's original intent for humanity. It carries the authority of a perpetual covenantal relationship. The remainder of this book reveals how humanity, beginning with Adam and Eve, failed to uphold this critical covenant. The consequences directly and immediately impacted the blessing God had bestowed upon them. In the chaos that followed, subsequent generations lost sight of the covenant. This has allowed Satan to steal, kill, and destroy resources intended for God's Kingdom on a scale that we can scarcely comprehend. And he has used these stolen resources for a specific purpose.

That, my friend, is where we find ourselves today.

---

[9] Genesis 4:12

Chapter 3
The Covenant Broken

> "You shall not eat from it or touch it, or you will die."
> Genesis 3:3b

God is a master strategist. He has always had a plan to accomplish His will through His imperfect image bearers. The covenant established at Creation is how He ensured we would have the material and human resources needed to build a global Kingdom. As I chronicled in Part 1 of *"I Came to Give,"* the principles of cooperation, stewardship, abundance, protection of human identity, and sustainability are the economic framework that God intended for us to adopt so that we could *maintain* that covenant.[10]

Unfortunately, Satan is also a strategist. It is no surprise then, that he directly and strategically created counters to those principles to achieve *his* desired outcomes. Chapter two of *I Came to Give*[11] details how he does this by revealing his motivation and skill set. Knowing this will help followers of Jesus effectively maneuver on today's economic battlefield. For the purposes of this book, I will provide a highly condensed summary of a profile, with multiple references to Scripture and *I Came to Give,* of the one we call…

---

[10] *I Came to Give* and *My Ways*, Doug Tjaden
[11] *I Came to Give*, Chapter 2, "I Will…", Doug Tjaden

The Thief

Ezekiel 27 and 28 reveal that, at one time, Satan occupied a privileged position in God's inner court.[12] It was there that he developed and perfected his skills in trade.[13] He was cast from heaven because he used those skills to acquire what was not given to him to use for his purposes, rather than God's.[14] Satan then declared his intent to assume the position, person, and purpose of God *and build a competing kingdom of his own on earth*.[15] Because he owns nothing,[16] he formulated a specific strategy to leverage his skills in trade to steal, kill, and destroy[17] the resources intended to build God's Kingdom and redirect them for his purposes.

During his time in heaven, Satan had become a master in economic development and trade. This is why God warned Adam to "keep" the garden before the Fall. He knew of Satan's skills. He knew of his plans. He knew that the only way for Satan to succeed was to undermine the covenant that would provide God's people with resources in such abundance that Satan stood no chance at accomplishing his objectives.

As we continue examining Scripture, we see in Genesis 3 that Satan wasted no time. He selected his target and put his well-honed skills into practice.

> "¹Now the serpent was more crafty than any beast of the field which the LORD God had made. And he said to the woman, 'Indeed, has God said, "You shall not eat from any tree of the garden?" ²The woman said to the serpent, "From the fruit of the trees of the garden we may eat; ³but from the fruit of the tree which is in the middle of the garden, God has said, "You shall not eat from it or touch it, or you will die.""'
> Genesis 3:1-3

Notice that in verse three, God defines a specific term of the covenant He established between humanity and Creation in the first

---

[12] Ezekiel 28:14-15
[13] Ezekiel 27:2-3a; Ezekiel 28:1-5
[14] Ezekiel 28:14-16
[15] Isaiah 14:13-14
[16] Psalm 50:10-12
[17] John 10:10

Chapter 3: The Covenant Broken

two chapters. It, a) defines an action (stay away from the tree) and, b) spells out the consequences of violating the action (you will die). Satan's strategy was to entice Eve to create the greatest possible damage to the relationships between God, Jesus, humanity, and Creation. As we know, he executed it flawlessly.

> "The serpent said to the woman, 'You surely will not die! For God knows that in the day you eat from it your eyes will be opened, and you will be like God, knowing good and evil. When the woman saw that the tree was good for food, and that it was a delight to the eyes, and that the tree was desirable to make one wise, she took from its fruit and ate; and she gave also to her husband with her, and he ate."
> Genesis 3:4-6

While in no way do I praise Satan, I must acknowledge the success of his strategy. He used his negotiating skills as a master tradesman to manipulate Eve into breaking the terms of the covenant. Most people believe that Eve first sinned when she bit the fruit. However, the terms of the covenant clearly state that she was not allowed to *touch* it.

Therefore, when Eve reached out and plucked it from the tree, she took control of an item that God did not give her the legal authority to possess. In that moment, she relinquished the principle of *stewardship,* which directs us to use what is given to us for *God's* purposes and according to *His* desires. She illegally claimed *ownership* over it, using it for *her* purposes and according to *her* desires. Please do not miss what just happened here.

Satan strategically lured Eve to steal from God, making her what he is—a thief—for the very reason he became one—to "be like God."

Satan instigated the first act of theft in heaven. It got him banished from heaven. Eve instigated the first act of theft on earth. It got her banished from the Garden. Both violated a covenant between the parties to *steward* what God had given them, setting off a cascading series of events that produced consequences that have reverberated throughout history.

There is enough economic theory, strategy, and execution contained in this one encounter to write an entire book. And indeed, a great deal of *I Came to Give* is dedicated to unpacking it in a manner that any follower of Jesus and easily understand. In it, we see that the immediate consequences of Eve's theft were to simultaneously cause a break in relationship between humanity, Creation, and God. The following excerpt from chapter three of *I Came to Give* explains what happened next.

"God created a world where the first law of thermodynamics and inertia supported the exponential growth of His Kingdom. However, when sin entered the world, there was an immediate and profound change. That brings us to the second law of thermodynamics.

This law states that in the material world, when energy transforms from one form to another, some of it is wasted. Additionally, any structure, system, or machine that is created by transferring energy (create order) will immediately begin to degenerate (disorder). Scientists refer to this process as "entropy."

When Adam and Eve failed to "cultivate" (serve) and "keep" (protect) Creation, they violated the Kingdom Building Principle of stewardship. Their failure to steward it for its highest and best purpose forced a separation between Creation and God's imagers, subjecting it "unwillingly" to "futility." Creation now groans for deliverance from the bondage of entropy.[18] Therefore, Adam and Eve's consequences were directly tied to their role in bringing about this new reality."

(end excerpt)

Let's recap what we know so far.

1. God established a covenant between Himself, Jesus, Creation, and humanity. Its purpose is to tie all parties of the covenant together relationally to achieve God's desired outcomes.
2. The covenant provides the foundation of an economic system that enables humanity to steward the earth's resources, enjoy the blessings of Genesis 1:28, and build God's Kingdom on earth.

---

[18] Romans 8:19-23

Chapter 3: The Covenant Broken

3. God specified the terms of the covenant and gave Adam instructions for maintaining it so that Creation could provide the resources to produce that outcome.
4. Satan declared his intentions to use his skills in economics to build a competing kingdom on earth. This required him to acquire vast human and natural resources that he does not own and has not been given stewardship of.
5. Satan used his skills to entice Eve to break the covenant by stealing God's property. This fractured the relationships between all parties of the covenant, opening the door for Satan to steal, kill, and destroy resources that were intended to build God's Kingdom on earth and instead use them to build his.

Because God is just, the consequences of our poor choices are directly related to the sin committed. The first consequence prescribed for Eve relates to her part in breaking the covenant with Creation. From that day forward, every woman is reminded of Eve's sin as they bring into the world the human family needed to steward Creation and build God's Kingdom.

Her second consequence is related to taking control of the fruit to use it for her own purposes. She "ruled over" Creation in a manner God did not intend. As a result, she would be subject to Adam's desire to "rule over" her in a manner God did not intend.[19]

Adam's consequences were similarly related to the role he played in breaking the covenant. Stewarding Creation to provide for our families and build His Kingdom is orders of magnitude more difficult than God intended.

> "Because you have listened to the voice of your wife, and have eaten from the tree about which I commanded you, saying, 'You shall not eat from it'; Cursed is the ground because of you; In toil you will eat of it All the days of your life. "Both thorns and thistles it shall grow for you; And you will eat the plants of the field; By the sweat of your face You will eat bread, Till you return to the ground,

---

[19] Genesis 3:16

> Because from it you were taken; For you are dust, And to dust you shall return."
> Genesis 3:17b-19

Now, let's take a moment to address something that may seem trivial, but I assure you, it is not. Note that in describing the consequences of Adam and Eve's sin, I did not use the word "curse." That is because when we hear that word, we associate it with its definition: "An appeal or prayer for evil or misfortune to befall someone or something."[20] This implies that God appealed to a higher being or prayed for misfortune to befall Adam and Eve.

The most obvious problem with this is that God is the ultimate authority. He had no one to "appeal" or "pray" to. Second, God loves His human family! He did not use His power to *intentionally* cause evil and misfortune to befall them. Instead, He was greatly grieved that they sinned. Their hardship was not a result of God's "curse" but rather a natural consequence of their actions.

The following demonstrates why every "jot and tittle" in Scripture is so important. God said to Adam, "Cursed is the ground because of you…" The Hebrew word used is *ârar*. Grammatically, it can be used a number of ways. In this instance, it is a passive participle,[21] which describes something upon which *an action was previously taken*. For example, in the sentence "The broken window was repaired," the word "broken" is a passive participle because the window didn't break itself—*something happened to it*.

This distinction is important because in this verse it means God did not "curse" the ground in the *active* sense that the modern definition implies. Nor did God curse Adam or Eve. Read those verses again. Adam, Eve, and the ground were subjected to "evil and misfortune" *because of what Adam and Eve did*, which was to fail to honor their covenant with Creation.

I am concerned that many followers of Jesus believe that God, out of His anger, used His power to cause evil and misfortune to befall Adam, Eve, and Creation. I believe this contributes to our modern culture's view that it is better to do nearly anything other than become

---

[20] Websters Dictionary
[21] https://biblehub.com/hebrew/779.htm

Chapter 3: The Covenant Broken

a steward of Creation. Instead, like me, they go to universities and cities to find "a better life," and pursue "the American Dream."

As a result, today, many people take our farmers and ranchers for granted. Others see them like the shepherds in biblical times—as second-class citizens. Yet these beloved stewards provide our food, without which we would all die and there would be no such thing as "economic activity" and no Kingdom to build.

The Path Forward

Although we cannot return to the pre-Fall state of Creation, we can mitigate many of the consequences humanity has lived with since then. To do so, the body of Christ must understand Satan's strategy to steal, kill, and destroy God's Kingdom by controlling the systems that manage economic activity. *I Came to Give*, documents how, from Genesis to today, this strategy has been successful beyond Satan's wildest dreams. It has enabled him to inflict the maximum possible damage to humanity's relationship with God, Jesus, *and* Creation, clearing the path to continue his quest to build the dominant kingdom on earth and achieve his goal to "be like the Most High."[22]

The economic system we live with today is built according to a set of principles that directly oppose God's principles of cooperation, stewardship, abundance, protecting our identity as His image bearers, and sustainability. These "basic principles of the world"[23] are competition, ownership, scarcity, stealing, killing, and destroying our identity as God's image bearers, and efficiency.

Satan's principles have formed the cornerstone of his economic strategy from the moment he entered the Garden of Eden and lured Adam and Eve into using food to make an illegal trade and usher in the Fall. Over the entire course of human history, these principles have enabled the kings of the earth to insert themselves as a third party into every exchange of value between human beings and steal some, or all, of that value.

What follows is a brief overview of how these principles became entrenched in the world, dating all the way back to Genesis 4. This is

---

[22] Isaiah 14:13-14
[23] Colossians 2:8 NKVJ

where Satan first reveals his commitment to his strategy, and we discover the generational consequences of perpetuating our broken covenant. It will serve as a springboard to the next chapter, where we begin to count the cost of Satan's success over the millennia.

Scripture is silent on why Adam and Eve taught Cain and Abel to make offerings to God. A logical, yet admitted, speculation is that Adam and Eve were devastated by the consequences of breaking the covenant. They lived in a world where the blessings of the covenant surrounded them. One can only imagine the sorrow they experienced when that world disappeared before their eyes as a result of their actions.

Therefore, in repentance, they intentionally passed a ritual to the next generation that reminded them of the principles that would enable future generations to restore the covenant by cultivating and keeping Creation. They were to give thanks to the Creator and worship Him in awe and mercy for designing Creation to produce the abundance required to build His Kingdom despite the consequences of their sin.

Consider the fact that Cain's offering to God represented the abundance produced by stewarding day five of Creation, the land that produced plants to feed humanity and animals. Abel's offering represented the abundance produced by stewarding day six of Creation, the animals that would feed and clothe humanity. The three pre-Fall economic principles of cooperation, stewardship, and abundance would enable Cain and Abel to honor the covenant and make their offerings.

It is hard to imagine how difficult those first years of spiritual warfare were. Adam and Eve had spent time fully under God's protection. Suddenly, it was gone. Satan had just won a major victory. He was emboldened. He was skilled. He was determined to assume God's position, purpose, and person and "be like the Most High."[24] Yet, now he had at his disposal two new ruthless spirits—control and competition—to unleash and wreak havoc on the first family.

> "Then the LORD said to Cain, "Where is Abel your brother?" And he said, "I do not know. Am I my brother's keeper?" He said, "What have you done? The voice of your brother's blood is crying

---

[24] Isaiah 14:13-14

Chapter 3: The Covenant Broken

to Me from the ground. Now you are cursed from the ground, which has opened its mouth to receive your brother's blood from your hand. When you cultivate the ground, it will no longer yield its strength to you; you will be a vagrant and a wanderer on the earth."
Genesis 4:9-12

This passage contains several hidden, yet important, revelations. First, Satan's attack on the second generation was designed to continue undermining humanity's ability to keep the covenant. Second, when Cain killed Abel, it further defiled the land. The Hebrew word *ârar* is used again in this passage as a passive participle, indicating that this too was a self-inflicted "curse." Finally, note that God did not hear about the innocent blood Cain had shed from His human family, *but from the land.* We do not know how this communication actually happened, however, it does provide additional evidence of the active and intimate relationship God and Jesus have with Creation.

Unfortunately, unlike his parents, Cain remained unrepentant. Therefore, as he worked to cultivate and keep his garden, it did not produce the abundance it was capable of. Satan was thrilled with the success of his strategy. The covenant had been broken and Creation struggled to produce the resources needed to build God's Kingdom. From that point on, Satan had established his primary method of operation.

Driving a wedge between the participants of the covenant *by any means necessary* became his primary economic strategy to steal, kill, and destroy the value produced by God's people. Fast forward some two thousand years and, unfortunately, we see further evidence of his continued success.

> "Now it came about, when men began to multiply on the face of the land, and daughters were born to them, that the sons of God saw that the daughters of men were beautiful; and they took wives for themselves, whomever they chose. Then the LORD said, "My Spirit shall not strive with man forever, because he also is flesh; nevertheless, his days shall be one hundred and twenty years." The Nephilim were on the earth in those days, and also afterward, when the sons of God came in

to the daughters of men, and they bore children to them. Those
were the mighty men who were of old, men of renown."
Genesis 6:1-4

It is tempting to take some time and more fully explore Dr. Michael Heiser's teaching on the Nephilim in his book, *The Unseen Realm*.[25] However, for our purposes, it is sufficient to know that he references the book of Enoch, which describes how the "watchers" taught humanity to make weapons for war. This one act exponentially increased the ability of human beings to follow Cain's lead and defile Creation on a massive scale with innocent human blood. It also led both God and humanity to a point of no return.

"Now the earth was corrupt in the sight of God, and the
earth was filled with violence. God looked on the earth,
and behold, it was corrupt; for all flesh had corrupted
their way upon the earth."
Genesis 6:11-12

These two verses are a concise depiction of the state of the world after the successful execution of Satan's strategy for two thousand years. The amount of blood shed was enormous. Can you imagine the cacophony in God's ears of the cries from the blood that soaked the land? Along with groaning for redemption, *it demanded justice*. And God responded accordingly.

"Then God said to Noah, 'The end of all flesh has
come before Me; for the earth is filled with violence
because of them; and behold, I am about to destroy
them with the earth.'"
Genesis 6:13

We are all familiar with what happened next.

---

[25] Dr. Michael Heiser, *The Unseen Realm*

Chapter 4
The Cost

"When you cultivate the ground, it will no longer yield
its strength to you; you will be a vagrant and
a wanderer on the earth."
Genesis 4:12

Within two thousand years of the creation of man, humanity and the earth had been corrupted to the point that there was no practical path to restoration. Humanity had completely ignored their covenant to serve and protect Creation and to steward the abundant resources provided to build God's Kingdom. God's response was revealing.

Genesis 6:6 says He was *grieved* in His heart and *sorry* that He had made man. The Hebrew word for "grieved" is *âṣab*, and it indicates deep emotional pain. The Hebrew word for "sorry" is *nâḥam*, and it means to sigh as moved with compassion to repentance.

The intensity of God's lament reveals His deep love for His Son, humanity, and Creation. He was so overcome by the breakdown in the relationship between them, due to the fractured covenant, that He could no longer watch them continue to suffer the consequences. Something had to change. Therefore, God declared that He would establish a new covenant with humanity and Creation whereby He would ensure the circumstances that led to the need to destroy the world He loves, and its inhabitants,[26] would never again be repeated.

"I will establish My covenant with you; and you shall enter the ark—
you and your sons and your wife, and your sons' wives with you."
Genesis 6:18

---

[26] John 3:16

God's use of a global flood to destroy the earth allowed him to rid the earth of those who broke the covenant and *cleanse the shed blood from the land*. Both were necessary to restore a clean foundation from which humanity and Creation could begin again. This new beginning mirrored the original creation narrative in many ways. However, note that it also included new terms that were necessary for this new covenant to endure.

> "And God blessed Noah and his sons and said to them, 'Be fruitful and multiply, and fill the earth. The fear of you and the terror of you will be on every beast of the earth and on every bird of the sky; with everything that creeps on the ground, and all the fish of the sea, into your hand they are given. Every moving thing that is alive shall be food for you; I give all to you, as I gave the green plant. Only you shall not eat flesh with its life, that is, its blood. Surely I will require your lifeblood; from every beast I will require it. And from every man, from every man's brother I will require the life of man. Whoever sheds man's blood, By man his blood shall be shed, For in the image of God He made man. "As for you, be fruitful and multiply; Populate the earth abundantly and multiply in it.""
> Genesis 9:1-7

It is incredible that God had the foresight to design Creation in such a way that it could still produce in abundance after such a catastrophic event. Doing so enabled Him to restate humanity's original mission, given in Genesis 1:28—with some conditions.

Let's not lose sight of the fact that, after the flood, God took into account humanity's most consequential failures up to this point in history. He reminded Noah that Creation is His gift to humanity and that it will provide them with abundant food. He also informed Noah of specific and strict consequences of defiling the land through the shedding of innocent blood. Then God unilaterally established His new covenant with both humanity and Creation.

> "Now behold, I Myself do establish My covenant with you, and with your descendants after you; and with every living creature that is with you, the birds, the cattle, and every beast of the earth with you; of all that comes out of the ark, even

Chapter 4: The Cost

every beast of the earth. I establish My covenant with you; and all flesh shall never again be cut off by the water of the flood, neither shall there again be a flood to destroy the earth."
Genesis 9:9-11

The world was at a new beginning. Before we continue, let's take a moment and summarize a few key points that brought us to this point in the biblical narrative.

- When Adam and Eve violated the original covenant, their consequences were directly related to their stewardship of Creation and the production of resources necessary to build God's Kingdom on earth. Adam's consequences were tied to natural resources and Eve's to human resources.

- When Cain shed Abel's innocent blood, his consequence was that when he cultivated the ground, it would no longer "yield its strength." This left him wandering around the earth in search of food.[27]

- Humanity became so corrupt that violence and bloodshed became the normal way of relating to one another, creating a never-ending cycle of defiling the earth. God therefore had to begin anew.

- In the wake of the earth's destruction, God instituted a new covenant that ensured Creation would never again have to pay the ultimate price for fallen humanity's negligence.

It was indeed a new beginning. However, for Creation to produce the resources necessary to fulfill the restated mission of Genesis 1:28, humanity needed to repent and honor the original covenant. Serving and protecting the earth needed to be reestablished *as a centering point* for relationships between humans, God, Jesus, and Creation. Embracing God's economic principles of cooperation, stewardship,

---

[27] Genesis 4:12

abundance, protection of identity, and sustainability would ensure the covenant would be honored for generations.

Unfortunately, you do not have to read much further in Genesis to see that humanity failed again on all accounts. Economic systems once again became dominated by the enemy's principles of control, competition, ownership, scarcity, identity theft, and fragility. Ever since, humanity has struggled to build a system based on God's economic principles and fulfill our covenant to cultivate and keep Creation.

Today, the church has no idea the enormous cost to humanity and Creation that has resulted from continuing to embrace man's systems. It is mind boggling that followers of Jesus are content to adopt the economic principles of control, competition, scarcity, self, and fragility when we have clear scriptural and historical evidence of the destruction they heap on humanity and the earth. Yet the church stubbornly continues to embrace these traditions of men. As a result, we suffer the self-inflicted "curse" of making the "Word of God of no effect" as all kinds of evil is unleashed in our families, churches, and communities—and on Creation.

We now live in a world where war, abortion, and cultural genocide committed against indigenous people have spilled so much innocent blood that the cries from the earth once again continually fill God's ears. Adding to the "curse," aggressive tilling practices and mono-crop farming have been adopted worldwide over the last century.[28] Now, what was once deep, lively, nutrient-rich topsoil has become shallow and nearly dead.

Today, much of the world's farmland acts only as a temporary holder for root systems of genetically modified plants. Each requires a toxic brew of chemicals and artificial fertilizers to produce their yield. In effect, the land is being raped—forced to "give up its strength" against its will and natural use. As alarming as this is, it is just a small accounting of the earth's side of the cost ledger.

The cost to the human side of the ledger is staggering. Large corporate food production, processing, and distribution systems have

---

[28] https://www.sciencenews.org/article/soil-erosion-rate-us-midwest-unsustainable-usda

Chapter 4: The Cost

disconnected most humans from the intimate relationship God intended them to have with His Creation. They produce highly processed foods that are laced with additives and preservatives and provide little nutritional value. These systems are now central to a growing health crisis in nations worldwide that feeds fat profits to both "big ag" and "big pharma."

Adding to humanity's woes is the fact that most people rarely, if ever, touch the soil with the intention to cultivate and keep it. Instead, they have turned their attention to consuming "stuff" created by an economic system that has become efficient at extracting natural, non-reproducible elements from the land and converting them into products that provide little real utility value.

But what is even more concerning is what is happening with the development of AI. A well-established historical reality is that there is a direct correlation between human flourishing and access to energy. Yet today, data centers are being created to feed hundreds of terawatt hours of electricity into the AI beast. It seems the kings of the earth are more concerned with feeding computers than people.

This is just a small sliver of the brutal *economic* reality we live with today. The *cultural* reality is just as brutal. Take for example the precipitous decline of families gathering around the table to share meals. A study published in the *Journal of Adolescent Health* found that frequent family meals were associated with lower rates of depression and suicidal thoughts among adolescents.[29] Yet today, many busy and distracted parents no longer know the joy of preparing meals for their families. Instead, they consider it a burden to do so.

This is the direct result of losing our connection with the covenant God gave humanity in the Garden, and our failure to adopt His economic principles. Instead, we have become slaves to an economic system that is intentionally designed to steal, kill, and destroy the Kingdom of God while building a competing kingdom in its place. It is tragic that not only do most followers of Jesus fail to understand this, but the enemy's systems are embraced and celebrated by them for the "wealth" they enable them to create!

---

[29] Eisenberg, M. E., Olson, R. E., Neumark-Sztainer, D., Story, M., & Bearinger, L. H. (2004). Correlations Between Family Meals and Psychosocial Well-being Among Adolescents.

Let me be clear. I am not throwing stones here. My history of embracing the traditions of men is deep. My struggle to break free is real and continues to this day. However, as we move into an extended period of cultural, geopolitical, and economic uncertainty, it is becoming clear that God will not tolerate our continued ignorance of His Word and His ways. If humanity continues to embrace man's ways, God is not obligated to bail us out by supernaturally providing the resources necessary to avoid hardship. On the contrary. The Bible and history are clear. He will use hardship to lovingly get our attention. The question then becomes, how will we respond?

Start at the Beginning and Deal with Reality

The answer is not complex. It just takes repentance, courage, and commitment. The book of Genesis reveals basic principles that will solve difficult problems. It also reveals God's original intention for humanity, and Satan's strategies and tactics to disrupt those intentions. By knowing both, we will be equipped to understand the world around us and know how we, as followers of Jesus, should respond in these challenging days.

However, knowing and responding are two very different things. Moving from one to the other requires followers of Jesus to *do what will seem radical in the eyes of man.* It will require them to deal with reality as it is, not as they wish it to be. Both are a challenge in any culture that is steeped in man's traditions.

And that brings us to Part 2. It will not be an easy read for many. We have a monumental task ahead. Satan's strategy to employ the kings of the earth to design and dominate economic systems has not changed throughout history. He has been successful beyond his wildest dreams, and he will *not* give up his territory without a fight.

The next four chapters will make that point clear. However, please know that I did not write them to instill fear. Instead, they are given as a dose of reality to inoculate you *from fear*.

"Let no one deceive you with empty words, for because of these things the wrath of God comes upon the sons of disobedience. Therefore do not be partakers with them; for you were formerly darkness, but now you are Light in the Lord;

Chapter 4: The Cost

walk as children of Light (for the fruit of the Light consists in all goodness and righteousness and truth), trying to learn what is pleasing to the Lord. Do not participate in the unfruitful deeds of darkness, but instead even expose them; for it is disgraceful even to speak of the things which are done by them in secret. But all things become visible when they are exposed by the light, for everything that becomes visible is light. For this reason it says, "Awake, sleeper, And arise from the dead, And Christ will shine on you." Therefore be careful how you walk, not as unwise men but as wise, making the most of your time, because the days are evil. So then do not be foolish, but understand what the will of the Lord is."
Ephesians 5:6-17

God is on the throne. His love for us is secure. His Word and His ways will always overcome His adversaries. And He is moving powerfully on this earth *in this day* to restore His Kingdom. I encourage you to let this be your focus as you read the next chapters, and as you see events unfold around us in the coming years.

Part 2
Understanding the Times

Chapter 5
Reality Check

"…the sons of Issachar, men who understood the times, with knowledge of what Israel should do,"
1 Chronicles 12:32a

What follows are some of the most difficult chapters I have written in any of my books to date. Content creation was not the challenge, as there is plenty of source material on the subjects presented. The challenge, due to the diversity of the audience that will read this book, is that some will think I went too far while others will think I did not go far enough.

Therefore, at the outset, I want to acknowledge my humanity, biases, and the reality that my sources, while some of the best in the world, are not infallible. There is a tremendous amount of "noise" today in both the natural and supernatural realms. Therefore, I will do my best to lean into Scripture and history to apply what they say about our present circumstances to the context of this book's primary focus—our covenant with God and Jesus to steward Creation.

God tucked 1 Chronicles 12:32a inside a rather benign narrative detailing the gathering of David's supporters at Hebron, where they were preparing to make him king over all of Israel. It has become a well-known, and often quoted verse, because it is one of the most concise expressions of one of the most important principles in Scripture. The need to combine understanding with effective action, which begins with closing the gap between perception and reality.

One can recognize this "gap" by listening to what people say when uncomfortable circumstances present themselves. "Everything is fine," "Things are not that bad," "God will protect us," and "God is in control" are some of the most common refrains. The first two are often uttered from a position of naivety or ignorance. The latter two are often taken out of context, as they ignore the principles of personal responsibility and sowing and reaping. In the end, it is difficult, if not impossible, for those uttering any of them to accept truth that requires admitting reality is not as they wish it to be.

Unfortunately, as unfolding events reveal that someone has lost contact with reality, they still refuse to relent. They begin to rationalize the cognitive dissonance they experience through outright denial of indisputable facts. At some point, however, reality begins to manifest in their lives in a tangible way, often with catastrophic consequences. Sadly, this pattern has plagued humanity throughout history.

> "Is there anything of which one might say, 'See this, it is new'? Already it has existed for ages which were before us. There is no remembrance of earlier things; And also of the later things which will occur, There will be for them no remembrance among those who will come later still."
> Ecclesiastes 1:10-11

The Old Testament prophets widely understood the depth of wisdom and understanding behind Solomon's statement. They were students of God's ways and history. The prophets had read, heard, and understood the "it" Solomon spoke of—historical patterns of human beings collectively having "no remembrance of earlier things." They knew the consequences that followed from the tendency of people to embrace naivety and ignorance. The prophets cried from the rooftops, "See *it* and repent! Turn away from your embrace of man's ways!", only to have their cries answered with "No! This time, it is different!"

Unfortunately, in most of the Western world, we are witnessing the same pattern. The body of Christ has overwhelmingly given its jurisdiction over the stewardship of Creation to the kings of the earth via corporate farms (food creation), multinational food conglomerates (food processing and distribution), and big pharma (our bodies). We have also given them nearly complete control of the world's economic and monetary systems. This trend has been in place for at least a century. What that means for us today is that the law of inertia is in effect, and meaningful change will not occur quickly and not without expending a great deal of energy.

Chapter 5: Reality Check

What follows will not be pleasant to hear, especially for those who are in the rationalism/cognitive dissonance phase of denial. Two sections from my previous books will provide context for what I believe we will likely experience between now (2025) and the early 2030s. The first is from chapter twenty-three of *I Came to Give*, entitled "Embrace the Great Restoration."

"Except for the period after the Great Flood, the world's economic, political, and financial systems are being simultaneously shaken like never before. Over the next decade, the design of *every system* that manages the flow of goods and services will change. Economic models. Supply chains. Monetary systems. The implications are far more profound than anyone can imagine.

Most people will have no idea what brought us to this point in history. However, you now know it is in large part due to the inevitable destabilization of society, brought about by thousands of years of leaders and families choosing to embrace economic and monetary systems that violate God's principles.

The ekklesia should not have been unprepared as we arrive at this point in history. Local, national, and international leaders have warned us for decades of the fatal structural flaws in our financial system. In 2012, Dennis Peacocke wrote about a looming "Great Reset" in his book, *On the Destiny of Nations - Resolving our Economic Crisis*.

In 2014, I attended a meeting in Atlanta with him and a small group of Christian economists. For two days we discussed "the coming Great Reset of the global financial system." Using what we had learned from the '08 financial crisis, we began to formulate strategies around the ekklesia's role in preparing for a transition to a new system.

At the end of the meeting, one participant stood up and said, "For the first time, I have hope that we (the ekklesia) may have answers to these problems and that we might actually be able to do something about it." I left the meeting with a copy of Dennis's book; encouraged that we were finally ready to engage.

Yet here we are. It is upon us. However, the scope of this "Reset" has broadened to include geopolitical, economic, and cultural transformation on a scale that we did not anticipate in that meeting in 2014. That means God is up to something much more than just fixing a broken financial system. It also means the disruption to "normal" life will be even more pronounced than we anticipated.

For this reason, fear will be even more intense as global systems of all kinds are shaken to their core. Unfortunately, frightened people often embrace anything they believe will lead to a return to normalcy. Like the Israelites after escaping from Egyptian bondage, they will clamor for leaders who will take them back to Egypt's "familiar comfort." [30]

Like Moses, however, it is the responsibility of church leaders to press forward. Now is the time to *lead*. Embrace what God is doing and do not kick against the goads![31] Likewise, just as a young Joshua and Caleb insisted on pressing forward to take a land "flowing with milk and honey," today's younger generations are willing to press in and claim a new land filled with God's abundance.

Entering this new "promised land" will not be easy. The spiritual environment we now find ourselves in is more intense than at any time in our lives. Thankfully, people like Dennis have spent years studying historical patterns that emerge during times of great shaking. In his book, he outlines three general phases that mark the progression of this time of great transformation.

(end excerpt)

The next several pages in *I Came to Give* outline what to expect in each phase. For brevity's sake, I will simply list the titles of each phase.

Phase One
Economic Stagnation, Denial, and Insufficient Remedies

Phase Two
The Bridge Period Between the Old and New Normal

Phase Three
The New Normal

I invite you to read all of chapter twenty-three in *I Came to Give*. It serves as a refresher of Dennis Peacocke's prophetic words, written in 2012. They are playing out according to what one would expect

---

[30] Numbers 14:3-4
[31] Acts 26:14

Chapter 5: Reality Check

during a "Fourth Turning." The world is well into Phase One, as of the writing of this book, and will soon enter Phase Two.

The second excerpt is from a section entitled "Food and Local Sovereignty" in chapter seven of *My Ways*."

"The kings of the earth and their "Great Reset" are exposing the rot of man's ways. As they continue to press their agenda, communities must take steps to protect their economic sovereignty in order to thrive. A critical step is to secure a sustainable and reliable source of food. Unfortunately, over the last forty years, supply chains for the manufacture and distribution of goods of all kinds have been stretched across the globe.

That may be okay for cell phones and automobiles. A major disruption in their supply may create a significant inconvenience, but it does not threaten the very survival of humanity. However, the prolonged disruption of energy, water, and food products, does. Unfortunately, until recently, central government leaders have taken no interest in a public discussion about how to fix the broken global food supply chain. They prefer "solutions" that will continue to empower the large multinational corporations, their shareholders, and the financial system that created the failing system in the first place.

There is even more at stake here than most people want to admit. Henry Kissinger said the quiet part out loud over fifty years ago. "He who controls the food controls the people." As of the writing of this updated edition in 2025, the threat to the established global economic and monetary system and the plans for a "Great Reset" are under real threat for the first time. It would be a grave mistake to underestimate the lengths to which the kings of the earth will go to protect what they have built over the last century. And, if Kissinger is correct (and history says he is), the ekklesia and local leaders must take steps now to protect local economic sovereignty and the health and well-being of their citizens by re-establishing a secure local food supply chain."

(end excerpt)

These two excerpts summarize the times we live in. By now, some of you may feel uncomfortable or even disagree with me. I understand. So, for the moment, let's assume that we will somehow escape the reaping phase of sowing into an abomination of an economic and monetary system for centuries, and God shows the world a Ninevah level of mercy. Scripture makes a strong theological case for the church to step up and implement systems based on God's principles and ways because they are designed to bless humanity in good times, bad times, or end times. The titles of my books came directly from Scripture for that very reason, and the sub-titles provide the context in which the titles are to be understood and applied.

I Came to Give
Understanding the Great Reset and The Coming Age of Abundance

My Ways
A New Economic Worldview For the 21st Century Ekklesia

Cultivate and Keep
An Economic Foundation for the Great Restoration

Each was written for the followers of Jesus all over the world. They provide the "ekklesia," (which is the Greek word translated as "church" in the New Testament and means "a governing body") with biblical support for taking up this cause and advancing it in the marketplace of ideas.

The "age of abundance" I refer to in the sub-title of *I Came to Give* is not present, but in the future. It is not yet our present reality because the ekklesia has failed to govern over economics and instead gave the jurisdiction of our economic and monetary systems to the kings of the earth. The "abundance" those systems have produced in Western economies and much of the developed world is largely an illusion because of the gross distortion of what Jesus meant by an abundant life. Nowhere in the Bible, let alone in Jesus' teachings, will you find abundance defined as a life filled with stuff, yet devoid of meaningful relationships, including with Creation.

Because the church has adopted the traditions of men and failed to heed God's economic ways for centuries, the ekklesia must take a long, hard look at this reality and make some serious adjustments to its "economic worldview." My three-book series is, in part, what God has asked me to contribute to the adjustment process. However, words in a book will not accomplish what must be done. In fact, as A.W. Tozer

Chapter 5: Reality Check

explains in *The Pursuit of God*, God's Word, *in isolation*, is not even sufficient to prompt meaningful change.

"The Bible is the written word of God, and because it is written, it is confined and limited by the necessities of ink and paper and leather. The voice of God, however, is alive and free as the sovereign God is free."

"God's word in the Bible can have power only because it corresponds to God's word in the universe. It is the present Voice that makes the written Word all-powerful. Otherwise, it all would be locked in slumber within the covers of a book."

"This universal voice of God was what the ancient Hebrews often called 'Wisdom,' and was said to be everywhere sounding and searching throughout the earth, seeking some response from the sons of men."

God's "economic wisdom" is revealed through His written Word, the historical record, *and* His present voice. God is seeking a "response from the sons (and daughters) of men." That response includes the creation of a framework for God's people to apply the wisdom of a biblical economic worldview in their families and communities.

Our response will come within the context of our present-day reality. There is tremendous inertia behind man's monetary and economic systems. The energy that created this inertia comes from the highest levels of principalities ever unleashed upon humanity. The energy required to *break* that inertia and set a new course is beyond what we can imagine. That means we must recognize the urgency to begin *now*.

> "So Jesus was saying to those Jews who had believed Him, "If you continue in My word, then you are truly disciples of Mine; and you will know the truth, and the truth will make you free."
> John 8:31-32

The truth of God's Word, principles, and ways contain more than enough spiritual "energy" to overcome inertia and change the course of human history. However, the context of this passage is sobering. Jesus spoke the truth. "Those with ears to hear" *and act on that truth* would be set free. Unfortunately, the "hearers" responded by accusing Jesus of being an illegitimate child who was demon possessed. When He gave them the whole truth, "…before Abraham was born, I am," they picked up stones to kill Him.[32]

Often, many followers of Jesus today are like the Jews in John 8. They seek the truth, yet they stop when a "truth" forces them to become the agents that deploy the spiritual "energy" needed to break inertia and change the world. We see the opposite modeled in Scripture. David and Solomon relentlessly sought God's truth and wisdom in the Psalms, Proverbs, and in Ecclesiastes.

Rarely were they satisfied with the first answers they found. Their insatiable appetite for "the whole truth" caused one to be forever known as "a man after God's own heart"[33] and the other as "the wisest man to live."[34] The apostles Peter and Paul shared their passion for truth. It filled them with the wisdom needed to lead a movement that "turned the world upside down."[35] David, Solomon, Peter, and Paul all understood the times in the context of *their present reality*. And their dedication to God's ways led them to know what to do.

And that brings me to the point of the next three chapters. God wants you to know the whole truth. You need to understand today's present reality. That means looking closely at the deep systemic problems in our economic, monetary, and agricultural systems. It means understanding the tremendous inertia behind these entrenched systems and the misguided principles they are built upon.

So, the challenge begins. The kings of the earth, and their secular business counterparts are well entrenched in their positions. The good news is that the power of God's Word and the present voice of our Creator are available to bring forth ideas and solutions that the kings of the earth cannot comprehend. So, while the pathway to this "age of abundance" will be bumpy, we have the hopeful expectation that we can navigate it and arrive at God's intended destination for humanity.

---

[32] John 8
[33] 1 Samuel 13:14
[34] 1 Kings 4:29-34
[35] Acts 17:6 (NKJV)

Chapter 6
Monetary Reality

> "Your silver has become dross, Your drink diluted with water. Your rulers are rebels And companions of thieves; Everyone loves a bribe And chases after rewards. They do not defend the orphan, Nor does the widow's plea come before them."
> Isaiah 1:22-23

Economic and monetary systems occupy a unique position in the world. They manage and unleash the "economic energy" that builds kingdoms—either for good or for ill. To understand why it is important for the ekklesia to take jurisdiction over these systems, you must first understand the principles behind the design of our present systems and the outcomes they produce. *I Came to Give* and *My Ways* addressed them in detail. What follows are the key concepts introduced and the assertions that are made in each book. For those who have read them, this will serve as a refresher.

Let's begin by acknowledging that, as followers of Jesus, our responsibility is to use the gifts and talents God gave us as His image bearers, along with Creation's natural resources, to build and advance His Kingdom. To "understand the times" and what we must do to accomplish this, we must redefine "economics" in Kingdom terms rather than what we have been taught by the academics set in place by the kings of the earth to validate their systems. With that in mind, I submit the following as a Kingdom-oriented definition.

"[Economics is] God's image bearers and His spiritual council working together with Him to serve, protect, and steward Creation's abundant resources and engage in trade that will protect human identity while advancing the Kingdom of God on earth."

This definition gives us a new standard by which to examine all economic and monetary systems. It comes down to answering two simple yet powerful questions.

- Do the systems support or hinder the ability of God's people to "cultivate" and "keep" Creation and maximize its ability to produce resources that will advance God's Kingdom?

- Do the systems prioritize the use of resources to protect and nurture the emotional, physical, and spiritual well-being of humans over the generation of material wealth?

The first question addresses how the systems manage natural resources, and the second, human resources. Answer these questions, and you will know whether followers of Jesus should embrace that system. When asking these questions about today's systems, you likely already know the answers. For our purposes, let me take a few minutes and provide an overview of the dysfunction of our economic and monetary systems as gleaned from *I Came to Give*, and *My Ways*.

Money From Hell

It is difficult to summarize the enormous gap between the principles that define our present monetary system and God's principles. To understand the full reality of what is presented here, you will need to read (or reread), chapter thirteen of *I Came to Give*, which shares the title of this section.

The problems with kings of the earth dominating the design of economic systems began long before the 21st century. Although Satan first gained control of the world's economic system when he tempted Eve to engage in an illegal trade, he gained his greatest advantage when the money used within the system began to be represented by metal coins. The prophet Isaiah foretold of where this would lead in one of the most widely overlooked prophecies in Scripture.

> "To whom will you liken Me, and make Me equal And compare Me, that we should be alike? They lavish gold out of the bag, And weigh silver on the scales; They hire a goldsmith, and he makes it a god; They prostrate themselves, yes, they worship."
> Isaiah 46:5-6 (NKJV)

Chapter 6: Monetary Reality

In 600 B.C., coins used in trade began to bear the image of animals, fulfilling Isaiah's prophecy. This single act set in motion a series of events that ultimately led governments to stamp coins with the images of "gods" and men who claimed to be gods. This is a critical turning point in economic history because it violated the first three of the Ten Commandments.

> "You shall not make for yourself an idol, or any likeness of what is in heaven above or on the earth beneath or in the water under the earth. You shall not worship them or serve them; for I, the LORD your God, am a jealous God, visiting the iniquity of the fathers on the children, on the third and the fourth generations of those who hate Me."
> Exodus 20:4-5

The spiritual implications of stamping money with the "likeness" of gods worshiped by the people are staggering. It embedded a generational curse in the economic system. The demonic forces associated with this new system helped them to continually design creative new ways to steal from the people and control them.

Over the centuries, Satan expanded his influence over the method by which money was created and issued around the world. His most diabolical scheme was born in China. For thousands of years, the Chinese had paid homage to the spirits of dead ancestors by ritually burning valuable gifts such as gold, silver, copper, and silk. Early in the seventh century, this demonic practice[36] enabled Satan's monetary princes to convince the Chinese people that instead of burning items of genuine value in their rituals, they should try substituting "religious paper" instead.

Paper was easy to make and cost little compared to precious metals and silk; therefore, the practice grew in popularity, and the use of religious paper spread rapidly. To appease their gods, the Chinese inscribed their paper with images and inscriptions of the items that they replaced: gold, silver, copper, and silk. Soon, the demonic spirits convinced the Chinese people that they *preferred* paper sacrifices over tangible items. In one such event, it is recorded that the spirits said, "I

---

[36] Deuteronomy 18:9-13, 1 Samuel 28:3

have no use for your copper cash; I desire cash only made from white paper."[37]

Using religious paper to represent "value" was Satan's opening gambit to capture control of the global monetary system. He rewrote the terms of the Chinese monetary system to include a form of "money" that could be easily manipulated and produced in unlimited quantity. Soon, "paper money" expanded beyond ritual use and become widely accepted in Chinese culture.

Over the next one thousand years, the use of paper money spread across Asia and into Europe. In 1690, it found its way to the United States. For the next three hundred years, paper money became a global standard. The historical record details how the kings of the earth became skilled at "debasing"[38] both their coins and paper money to deceitfully steal their citizens' wealth without detection.

Unfortunately, the historical record also shows that in nearly every case where governments allowed the debasement of money to become systemic, it led to the debasement of the minds of the nation's citizens.[39] Debased minds led to the corruption of culture and political institutions. Ultimately, the result was nearly always a collapse of the monetary system, the culture, and the government that began the debasement.

An excerpt from *I Came to Give*, chapter eighteen, entitled "From Paper to Debt," provides insights into how this trail of deceit led to the system we have today. A system that enables the kings of the earth and their cohorts to steal from, kill, and destroy on a massive scale those who are enslaved by it.

"Our present monetary system creates monetary items, not by pouring metal or even printing paper, *but when a bank makes a computer entry on a keyboard.* That keyboard entry creates a new loan to an individual, business, or government. Each unit of money you have in your possession represents a debt owed by someone else. The implications of this are difficult for most people to grasp until they realize:

---

[37] *A Study and Translation of Tang Lin's Ming-Pao Chi*, pg 254
[38] *Doug Tjaden, I Came to Give*, pg 155
[39] Romans 1:28

Chapter 6: Monetary Reality

Today's monetary system makes nearly everyone a debt slave.[40]

It takes some time to comprehend the implications of that statement, and it is likely worse than you think. Let me explain.

The central government borrows money created by the banking system. It uses the money created with those keyboard strokes to fund much more than infrastructure and programs like social security and health care. It also regularly *enters trading floors* with organizations that perpetuate *all sorts of evil*. Abortion. Unjust war. Modern-day bread and circuses. And the list goes on…

That is not the worst of it. *You* are indirectly brought onto those trading floors. A portion of your economic energy goes to them in the form of taxes, and *you cannot say "no."* Through tax laws, the government forces you to "strike surety" for its debt. Scripture is clear on this subject.

> "Do not be among those who give pledges, among those who become guarantors for [someone else's] debts."
> Proverbs 22:26

If you object and refuse to pay your taxes, the government will seize your property. If you continue to hold your position, your new home will either be on the streets or in prison. That is the definition of a debt slave.

Now, let me be crystal clear. I do not encourage you to become a tax protestor and refuse to pay your taxes. To do so would be pointless and foolish. The kings of the earth will always have their monetary systems. As you will discover in Part 3 of this book, we should focus our energy elsewhere. Therefore, Jesus' advice to Peter, "however, so that we do not offend them…" still holds true today.

As a member of the ekklesia, it is your responsibility to know the terms of today's monetary social contract. This book was written in part to expose a system that is currently draining you of resources that were meant to build the Kingdom of God. Absent this knowledge, you

---

[40] Proverbs 22:7

are powerless to change the terms and create a new system based on God's principles. Regardless of whether you are a national leader, mother, father, or young adult, you now have an opportunity to participate in changing those terms.

The need to make these changes has taken on a new sense of urgency. In 2020, the world took on *trillions* of dollars of new debt to counter the economic downturn associated with a pandemic. The enormity of this new debt has pushed the global debt-based monetary system to the verge of collapse. All debt-based monetary systems contain a structural flaw that makes a collapse unavoidable. The following illustration will demonstrate why:

- A bank extends you a personal loan for $10,000 at 5% interest. It is a balloon loan, with payment of the principal and interest due one year later.
- The $10,000 is created and given to you when you sign the loan papers, and an entry is made in the bank's computer.
- One year later, you owe $10,500.
- That $500 in interest must be paid with debt-based money.
- As a result, somewhere, a person, business, or government must create a loan so that the money to pay the interest can come into existence.
- A person, business, or government then owes interest on that new $500 of debt.

Now, consider that all the world's money is created through the issuance of debt. Interest accrues on the debt. Therefore, the system must issue a constant supply of new debt to create new money to service the interest on the money already in circulation. This cycle *never* ends. Both debt and the supply of money must always continue to expand. If it stops, the system will collapse in a massive downward spiral of debt defaults.

This is the description of a Ponzi scheme.

Chapter 6: Monetary Reality

You may ask, "Can't people and governments just pay off their loans?" Actually, no. Where will they get the money to pay back both the principal and interest? It would have to be created using... debt. Even if it were possible, paying off a loan causes the money that was created when it was issued to *disappear*. That means if everyone paid off their loans, the entire money supply (except paper cash and coins) would vanish. The system is insane.

This Ponzi scheme structure of debt-based monetary systems requires a *companion economic system to ensure continual economic "growth."* It does not matter what the economy produces. It could be cars or computers—or pornography. With a debt-based monetary system in place, the economy *must* grow to service the new debt issued to do what? Provide money to grow the economy!

If growth stops, or worse yet, the economy goes into recession (shrinking output) or depression (demand destruction), businesses will fail and default on their loans. People will default on their credit cards. And guess what? Debt defaults have the same effect as if the loans are repaid. The money disappears!

This reality has left today's central banks in a major bind. They must inject hundreds of billions or *trillions* of dollars whenever an external shock threatens to slow the economy. And during these downturns, who is the primary borrower that the system relies on to "stimulate" the economy? The central government? That is what bankers and government officials tell us. However, the "borrower of last resort" is *you,* the taxpayer.

This system is fundamentally flawed, and it is evil.

Since the financial crisis of 2008, the world's central banks have been working overtime to hold this scheme together. The recent pandemic and geopolitical turmoil have done nothing but magnify the problem. The system is close to its saturation point. The central bankers recognize the need to transition to a new system before losing control of the monster they created. The question is, how will they do it, and under what economic conditions?

(end excerpt)

This is the "monetary reality" that we live with today. I trust that this helps you better understand the increasing instability in our financial system, debased minds in our culture, and government corruption. Historical precedent leads us to conclude that we are possibly, if not likely, facing the prospect of the collapse of all three. I say again, it is time for the ekklesia to step up, "understand the times," and "know what we should do."

Chapter 7
Economic Reality

> "Those who practice such things will not
> inherit the Kingdom of God."
> Galatians 5:21b

Understanding the evil that produced our present monetary system is one thing. It is quite another to accept that our present economic system is a "necessary companion" to perpetuate that evil. Therefore, I need to state at the outset something that many people are going to find hard to accept. Capitalism is not God's answer to the economic tyranny and oppression being thrust upon humanity by the kings of the earth. In fact, as practiced today, it contributes to it.

Ouch. That assertion has caused the greatest push-back of anything I say or write. However, by the end of this chapter, you will see that capitalism is, in fact, designed to steal from and enslave humanity. It just goes about it in a much more insidious manner than socialism. Support for this assertion is covered extensively in *I Came to Give*, chapter nineteen, entitled "Economics - Meet Charles Darwin." The following excerpts will help set the context for the remainder of this chapter.

"Most people in the Western world are taught, since they are old enough to run a lemonade stand, that 'Capitalism is the best economic system ever devised by man. It has created more prosperity and lifted a greater number of people out of poverty than any other economic system in history.' This is true. However, let's examine more closely how and why it achieved this distinction.

First, the statement, "it is the best system ever devised by *man*," carries undertones of humanism for a reason, as you will soon learn. Second, the claim that capitalism has "lifted a greater number of people out of poverty than any other economic system," while technically accurate, is only because of opportunity. Although many nations today have adopted some form of capitalism, none have adopted an economic system based solely on the Principles of Kingdom Building.

I submit that if we could compare the production of abundance (according to Jesus' definition) in the early church with that produced by today's form of capitalism, I believe God's system would prove to be vastly superior on a per-capita basis. The official definition of capitalism will help us understand why:

"[Capitalism is] an economic system characterized by private or corporate ownership of capital goods, by investments that are determined by private decision, and by prices, production, and the distribution of goods that are determined mainly by competition in a free market."

Capitalism was initially built upon several core principles. The first two are:

- Private ownership of the means of production (capital goods).
- Free choice in what to produce, whom to sell to, and at what price.

Now we come to a major reason that I wrote the first eighteen chapters of [*I Came to Give*]. They established a theological and historical framework to understand the damage inflicted on humanity when the spirits of control and competition drive humans to act out of fear of scarcity. I have addressed the spirit of control and its relationship to socialism. Now it is time to turn to the spirit of competition and its relationship to capitalism.

As difficult as it may be for many to accept, competition and ownership, as understood and practiced by many, if not most followers of Jesus, are the leaven in capitalism. Unfortunately, this leaven has so thoroughly permeated the system that competition is now *the* primary driver behind capital creation and acquisition, as well as management of the flow of goods and services. Furthermore, ownership has

Chapter 7: Economic Reality

replaced stewardship, turning the heart inward to deploy the fruit of competition to serve the "owner," who we see as ourselves. Meanwhile, the bride of the true owner of *everything* – the Lord Jesus Christ—settles for leftovers given in the form of tithes and offerings.

Over the last century, competition in the marketplace has become so intense that businesses still operating today are seen as the "winners" in a marketplace game characterized by "survival of the fittest." This "neo-Darwinian" form of capitalism has become so pervasive that it influences how humans relate to one another in nearly every aspect of life."

(end excerpt)

An extremely illuminating documentary on economics and "marketing" is a four-part series released in 2002 by the British Broadcasting Company entitled *The Century of the Self*. There is a comprehensive review of the first hour, entitled "Happiness Machines"[41] in *I Came to Give*. It documents how Edward Bernays, nephew of Sigmund Freud, worked with businesses, banks, and the government to change people's buying habits by manipulating their perceived identities. The following excerpt touches on some of the more startling revelations in the documentary.

"Before Bernays entered the picture, advertising concentrated on *providing information* to influence buying behavior. Facts meant something. However, when Bernays returned to the United States, he took advertising in a new direction. He started the first "public relations" company in New York, using Freud's ideas to create a framework to make money by manipulating the "unconscious thoughts" of the masses.

Bernays crafted messages to alter how human beings viewed themselves. He believed that if you could get people to connect their identity to a product by manipulating their emotions, you could get them onto a trading floor where they would hand over their hard-earned money for nearly anything. It is easy now to see Satan's method of operation at work, is it not?

---

[41] *The Century of the Self* - "Happiness Machines"

The first broad-based public experiment Bernays undertook was to attack a long-standing and deeply embedded cultural taboo—women smoking in public. He approached the challenge by framing cigarette smoking as a symbol of male power. He then championed women who smoked publicly as challengers to male power and oppression. The tag line of his campaign? "Torches of freedom."

Bernays combined a deeply held value in the post-WWI culture (freedom) with an act of rebellion and manipulated women into believing that the two were the same. It directly appeals to Genesis 3:16b: "Yet your desire will be for your husband." The goal was to separate women from their identity as free imagers of God and then enslave them through an addiction that undermined their physical, emotional, and spiritual well-being.

It worked. Soon it was socially acceptable for women to smoke in public. In reality, it had nothing to do with rights or equality. Bernays simply did it as an experiment to manipulate humans through *feelings* and separate them from their identity. The cigarette companies stood ready to capture these orphaned women and turn them into cigarette buying machines. His experiment was diabolical in both design and execution.

With his first commercial "success" behind him, Bernays broadened the number of markets in which to deploy his scheme. He created advertising messages that linked irrelevant products to the *image* people wished to project. It did not matter whether the image was a lie. All that mattered was that it increased their status with their friends or within the community.

Soon companies created new magazines to promote specific images that men or women wanted to project of themselves. Film stars began to endorse products. Moviemakers began to place products in predominant scenes in their films. Car manufacturers made their products a symbol of male sexuality. Women were encouraged to express themselves through their clothing. As a result, throughout the early 1920s, huge new department stores were established across the nation to accommodate the demand produced by this new exploitation of capitalism…

Chapter 7: Economic Reality

...Slowly but surely, free will and the ability to resist marketing machines and social pressure became a thing of the past.[42] The spirit of competition set off an identity war. People connected their self-worth to their ability to proudly flash the latest toys and show that they lived the "American Dream" better than their neighbors. Today, businesses have made an art out of connecting people's identities to their corporate brand. From sneakers to cell phones, the logo is often now more important than the utility value of the product.

Friends, it is all just one giant manipulation by Satan to separate us from our identity as God's imagers and stewards of Creation. As soon as we fall prey to it, we repeat Eve's sin. We reach out and take control of what was never ours, claiming ownership for our own purposes. At that moment, Satan wins. He deceives us into thinking we deserve to build our own little kingdom where we selfishly devour the fruit of our labor.[43] Our economic energy then builds his kingdom.

I trust you now clearly see the spirits of control and competition at work in both socialism and capitalism. Satan is happy to let us argue about which is better, as both accomplish his goals of image separation, ownership, environmental destruction, and destruction of family, community, and national identity. In so doing, both systems separate us from access to the wealth and abundance that the true owner – our Lord and King Jesus Christ – intended for us all to enjoy. It is time to stop falling for Satan's trap and admit that both socialism and [capitalism are disastrous for God's Kingdom]."

(end excerpt)

The remainder of the documentary is equally fascinating—and heartbreaking. Bernays' ideas on how to manipulate the masses were adopted by Ernest Dichter, who took them to an entirely new level. He focused on controlling people by analyzing and manipulating their self-image—in short, *by stealing their identity*.[44] Dichter had two primary outcomes in mind. First, to make the masses docile and compliant. Second, to make them voracious consumers.

---

[42] https://bettermarketing.pub/free-will-willpower-are-becoming-a-thing-of-the-past-heres-what-you-can-do-about-it-58799091fb8a
[43] Luke 12:13-21
[44] *The Century of the Self* - "The Engineering of Consent"

Politicians quickly adopted the techniques Dichter used in the marketplace. Over the next several decades, the spirits of control (politicians) and competition (businesses) joined forces. They used "psychoanalysis," "public relations," and "motivational research" to manipulate and control human beings on a scale unprecedented in history.

Through control of today's political class and their bureaucracies, the enemies of God have taken jurisdiction over the design and management of the world's economic and monetary systems. When we overlay this reality with Scripture and biblical principles, it is heartbreaking to see the catastrophic impact the "Century of the Self" has had on the advancement of God's Kingdom on earth.

Will Not Inherit...

Followers of Jesus must have the courage to look at the historical record with clear eyes and an open mind. The world is experiencing a wave of global populism that is awakening the masses to the controlling spirit present in most national governments. However, as of this writing, few understand the "steal, kill, and destroy" design of neo-Darwinian capitalism, and its success in undermining the Kingdom of God. Why?

For generations we have been taught that economic "competition" is a godly principle that should be practiced by followers of Jesus. This has been so thoroughly accepted in Western culture that, until very recently, if you questioned capitalism, you earned swift public scorn. I have experienced that firsthand. When faced with it, my appeal is not to my books, but rather to the Scriptural support contained within them. When given the opportunity to let Scripture speak, the conversation can get awkward as cognitive dissonance sets in and those reading God's Word, *in context*, must deal with its uncomfortable truths.

I cover the subject of competition in much more detail in *I Came to Give* and *My Ways* than I will in this book. While I reference many scriptures to support the rather uncomfortable conclusion, it can be summarized by Paul's teachings in Galatians 5.

Most followers of Jesus are familiar with the "fruit of the Spirit" listed in verses twenty-two and twenty-three. However, prior to those,

Chapter 7: Economic Reality

Paul lists a set of specific behaviors that, in the context of the passage, are best labeled "the fruit of the flesh." They include:

Idolatry, strife, outbursts of anger, envy, drunkenness, disputes, dissensions, or factions.

I have a serious question. How many of these behaviors have you witnessed at sporting events? In my lifetime, I have not only witnessed them, but sadly, I have practiced many of them, both on and off the field. They are a byproduct of the elevated role competition plays in our sports-crazed culture. When I reflect on my experiences, I shudder to consider what Paul says right after listing these behaviors.

"Those who practice such things [idolatry, strife, outbursts of anger, envy, drunkenness, disputes, dissensions, or factions] will not inherit the Kingdom of God."
Galatians 5:21b

Will not inherit the Kingdom of God.

Galatians 5:13-25 is an extremely sobering passage, on par with the traditions of men that Jesus spoke of in Mark 7:5-13. When scripture identifies *specific behaviors* that "invalidate the Word of God," or result in people who "will not inherit the Kingdom of God," it should set off a five-alarm fire bell in your spirit. You should beg God to show you how to avoid such things at any cost. However, because we have been steeped in the relative comfort of Western culture and are now surrounded by the philosophy of empty deceit, the alarm in our spirit is more like a text notification going off in the middle of a football stadium during the Super Bowl.

Let me get straight to the point. A full exposition on the subject of competition, in the context of the entirety of Scripture, reveals there is not a single verse or principle that directs or encourages competition *between God's people*. Nor is there a single example that produced a positive outcome when it occurred. Not one. Instead, followers of Jesus are to focus our competitive desires in one area, identified by Paul in Ephesians 6:12.

"For our struggle is not against flesh and blood, but against the rulers, against the powers, against the world forces of this darkness, against the spiritual forces of wickedness in the heavenly places."

Competition by followers of Jesus should only be directed at displacing the spiritual powers and principalities that have displaced God's principles and ways in every area of life. Yet, when it comes to stewarding and exchanging the value we create as God's image bearers, we ignorantly or willfully embrace neo-Darwinian capitalism. By doing so, we expose it all to the spirits of control and competition.

And the result? Just look at Western culture. Slick marketing and branding appeal to people's identities. They are enticed to exchange the truth of their identity as stewards of God's Creation, tasked with building His Kingdom, for the lie that their economic duty is to be a "consumer" of products and services that fulfill the desires of the flesh. All the while, neo-Darwinian capitalism feeds a companion monetary system that must make debt slaves of us all, or both systems will die.

My friend, the hard reality is that together, today's economic and monetary systems seek self-preservation, as they leave a vortex of unimaginable destruction, of both Creation and human beings, in their wake. *This has been Satan's "economic strategy" for thousands of years.* The magnitude of the damage is only now becoming apparent to those who have the eyes to see it.

Author and historian Carl R. Trueman picked up where *The Century of the Self* left off. In his book, *The Rise and Triumph of the Modern Self*, he documents the widespread destructive nature of identity manipulation in Western culture.

"[Today] we all live in a world in which it is increasingly easy to imagine that reality is something we can manipulate according to our own wills and desires and not something that we necessarily need to conform ourselves to or passively accept... in which human beings are called to transcend themselves, to make their lives into works of art, to take the place of God as self-creators and the inventors, not the discoverers, of meaning."

Trueman goes on to note...

Chapter 7: Economic Reality

"[This may] offer an explanation as to why human identity has become so plastic and statements such as "I am a man trapped in a woman's body" come to make sense. If the inner psychological life of the individual is sovereign, then identity becomes as potentially unlimited as the human imagination."

The Century of the Self documents the use of demonic trading floors, during the 1900s, that were used to engage in the theft of peoples' identities as image bearers of God, the theft of the fruit of their labor, and the gross misallocation of Creation's natural resources. *The Rise and Triumph of the Modern Self* documents the natural progression of such a system, which transformed our culture into one in which it became offensive to define a woman as "a human adult female."

It is absurd that followers of Jesus would embrace systems that produce these outcomes. Yet here we are in the third decade of the twenty-first century. Many well-meaning followers of Jesus have joined the kings of the earth to fashion "the greatest economic system devised by man" into a de facto golden calf. Like all idols, those who worship it have sown the seeds of their own destruction, those they influence, and even their own families.

But it doesn't stop there. They cheer on those who are exporting this abomination of an economic system to the rest of the world, exposing humanity to its many sorrows. The traditions of men, along with image carved money that bears the name of God in vain, have trapped them in bondage in more ways than they can imagine.

This is the economic reality we live with today.

It is time for followers of Jesus to stop hiding behind rationalizations and "economic theory" to justify our embrace of economic and monetary systems that are repugnant to the King of the Kingdom we seek to build. Yes, because we are citizens of God's Kingdom *and* the world, we must interface with their systems. However, followers of Jesus are commanded *to do better*. [45] We are called to create a system that does not compromise God's principles.

---

[45] John 18:36, Romans 12:2

One that will exist alongside man's systems and free us from the disastrous consequences we have experienced by embracing it, while creating a better world for all of humanity.

As the world undergoes massive shifts on a global scale, God is exposing the economic and monetary traditions of men for all to see. This provides us with a once-in-a-century opportunity to take our intended place as those called out to design, build, and govern the systems that manage the fruit of our labor, first within the church, then within our local communities.

Whether or not we choose to seize the moment will determine if the kings of the earth retain their position as gatekeepers of our economic and monetary systems for generations. It will determine whether the enemies of God continue to steal, kill, and destroy the fruit of our labor and use it to build Satan's kingdom, or whether a new system, designed according to God's principles and ways, delivers the age of abundance that Jesus came to give, and the Kingdom of God powerfully advances on the earth.

That is a dose of hard reality.

Chapter 8
Food Reality

"Joseph provided his father and his brothers and all his father's household with food, according to their little ones."
Genesis 47:12

After the last two chapters, it should be evident that the economic and monetary systems, designed by the kings of the earth, are indeed the root of "all kinds of evil."[46] For over a century, they have driven humans to extract and mismanage Creation's natural resources to produce an "abundance" of things that do little to advance the Kingdom of God. In a twist of irony, for the last twenty years, those same the kings of the earth have propagated the narrative that they are the only ones capable of saving Creation by tackling the existential threat of "climate change."

Their plan? A "Great Reset" of capitalism to align it with their seventeen "sustainable" development goals.[47] Like Satan's legions, who in Genesis 11 borrowed God's economic principle of cooperation to build the Tower of Babel, the kings of the earth have now set their sights on co-opting the principle of sustainability to advance their agenda. It is *critical* that the ekklesia not allow this to happen. Instead, it is our responsibility to help our communities apply God's economic principles in the context of a *biblical economic worldview*.

The principle of sustainability is one of the five principles that form the foundation of that biblical economic worldview. This principle is so vital to any post-Fall system that God incorporated it into the design of every natural ecosystem, revealing a profound truth.

---

[46] 1 Timothy 6:10
[47] https://sdgs.un.org/goals

The degree to which sustainability is present or absent in critical systems defines the quality of all life on earth over the long term. This is especially true of our food supply system, which is a direct by-product of natural ecosystems.

The Window of Viability

Many secular scientists are realizing that, rather than competition and "survival of the fittest," abundance and cooperation, immutable principles written into the very fabric of nature, are the principles necessary for any sustainable ecosystem to function. They list five key attributes that help define such a system.

- Diversity: From the beginning, God filled the earth with abundant natural organisms that differ in form and function.

- Efficiency: Various components of an ecosystem exist to enhance the throughput of what flows through them.

- Persistence: A diverse subset of organisms, known as replicators, consistently reproduce and maintain a stable population while remaining in balance with all other organisms.[48]

- Symbiosis: Two or more dissimilar organisms living and working together in more or less intimate association for the benefit of both.

- Resiliency: Multiple pathways serve the system's needs by creating a "flow network" to distribute critical resources and preserve it through unexpected external disturbances.

These attributes combine to create what biologists call "the window of viability."[49] Natural ecosystems maintain their resiliency by creating a healthy number of diverse pathways to distribute critical resources across the ecosystem. If too many pathways exist, resources wander inefficiently around the system while entropy takes its toll. The

---

[48] Addy Pross, *What is Life?*, Pg 75
[49] Robert W. Ulanowicz, *A Third Window: Natural Foundations for Life Beyond Newton and Darwin*, 2008

ecosystem stagnates and slowly dies. If too few highly efficient pathways exist, the system becomes fragile, and when entropy intervenes, the failure of a single critical pathway causes the ecosystem to collapse suddenly. The following diagram illustrates the relationship between these various factors.

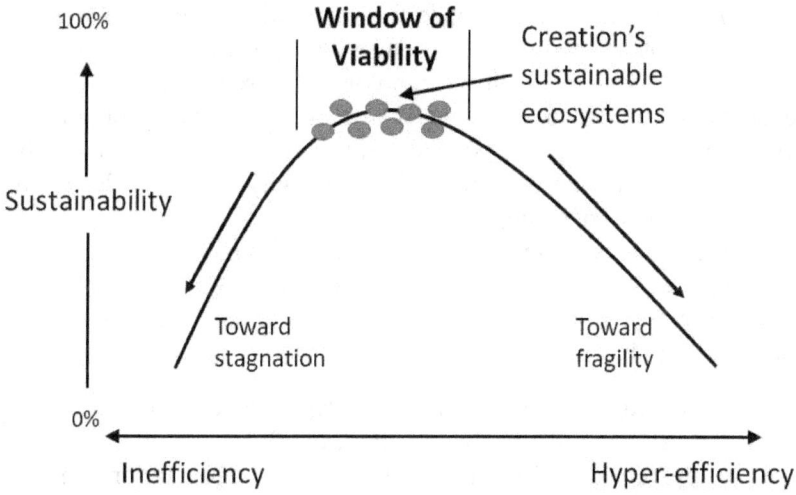

Having been raised on a farm, I witnessed firsthand the window of viability in action. It is the reason I am so concerned about what I see happening to the environment and the food supply chain today. Chris Cummings, national director of Colliers International's Food Advisory Group, published a paper in 2017 in which he stated that the present economic system's insatiable appetite for *efficiency* would impact the agricultural industry. He observed:

> "Every element of the food life cycle is ripe for accelerated change… The combined need for efficiency and innovation is drawing entrepreneurs and providing a perfect testing ground for emerging technologies for both food production and distribution."[50]

---

[50] https://www.colliers.com/en/news/food-fight-the-collision-of-technology-and-distribution-in-the-food-industry

Sure enough, fast forward to today. Technology is increasingly making its way onto the farm and firmly embedding itself in the global food supply chain. Fifty years ago, while sitting on a tractor with no cab and nothing but an AM radio, I could have never imagined today's monstrous equipment, controlled by GPS and computers that are more powerful than those that sent men into space in the 1960s.

The fact that different foods from around the world have found their way onto more tables, particularly in "developed" nations, is a perceived benefit of all this technology. Today much of the world expects that we can have any kind of food we want, any time of the year, delivered to supermarket stores just a few minutes from us. This is the result of the kings of the earth perfecting a highly efficient, yet complex, global food supply chain.

Unfortunately, as this system was being designed, developed, and implemented globally, unintended consequences were lurking on the horizon. Now those consequences are undermining the resiliency of our food supply.

- According to the United States Department of Agriculture (USDA), soil erosion affects around 24 billion tons of topsoil annually. This, along with urbanization and commercial land development, results in the loss of 1.5 million acres of farmable land each year.

- Because of the efficiencies created by economies of scale, mono-crop farming is now the norm for most commercial farmers. These farms concentrate on expertise, equipment, infrastructure, and yield, rather than soil health and longevity.

- Heavy use of chemical fertilizers and pesticides helped improve economies of scale. Higher yields and bulk purchases of seeds and specialized chemical fertilizers improved margins.

- These trends have combined to increase a farm's efficiency and size. The result has been a dramatic decrease in the number of farms. According to the United States Department of Agriculture (USDA), in 1935, there were 6.8 million farms in the United States. By 2021, the number decreased to 2 million.[51]

In the latter half of the "Century of the Self," these developments seemed like a blessing to a generation of children raised on farms, offering them a reason to escape from the physically demanding work of farming. In cities, they found high paying jobs, entertainment, and access to all kinds of identity-validating stuff just waiting to be consumed. The demonic lie sown in the spirit realm through the misinterpretation of the Genesis 3 "curses" contributed to a culture that now considers "cultivating" and "keeping" Creation to be a second-class occupation.

The evidence of this is pervasive. It does not matter whether you are in the United States, Europe, Latin America, Africa, or Asia. Rural communities struggle to survive. I have watched my little hometown of 280 souls change dramatically over the decades. In the late 1970s, it had a grocery store, a gas station, two repair shops, a diner, a lumber yard, a farm implement dealer, a blacksmith, a grain elevator, a school, a bar, a bank, and five churches.

Today, along with twenty percent of the population (the next generation), gone are the grocery store, the lumber yard, the blacksmith, the school, one of the repair shops, and three of the five churches. While a few new businesses have been added, most are connected to large corporations. Their profits are exported to the communities where their home offices are located and are of no benefit to the families remaining in my hometown.

It pains me to see this happen. However, my hometown is a microcosm of a global trend. Economic theories based on mathematical models and the traditions of men have maximized efficiency and profits at the expense of diversity, persistence, and symbiosis within the local economy. The resiliency of the economic ecosystem has been compromised, as it now depends on external corporations and corporate farms to provide jobs.

Meanwhile, the system harvested the next generation of farmers and sent them to the cities, breaking a centuries long tradition of passing the family farm from generation to generation. The result?

---

[51] USDA Economic Research Service: Family Farms.

Today, we are dependent on an increasingly fragile and highly concentrated system to supply humanity with the foundation for all economic activity in the world—the food that keeps us alive.

Food and the Spirit of Control

In the wake of the COVID-19 pandemic and increasing geopolitical and financial system instability, the world is discovering vulnerabilities in the global economic ecosystem. As mentioned earlier, oppressive governments regularly use food to control the people, maintain their dominance, suppress dissent, and advance their political agendas. The following are just three historical examples. There are many others.

The Holodomor in Ukraine, 1932-1933. The Holodomor was an artificial famine orchestrated by the Soviet Union under Joseph Stalin. By controlling access to food, the Soviet regime effectively crippled the Ukrainian population and their ability, or desire, to support any opposition to Stalin and his government. The Soviet government successfully suppressed Ukrainian nationalism and solidified its control over the nation. The cost was a catastrophic loss of life, with millions perishing from starvation.

Siege of Leningrad, World War II, 1941-1944. German forces laid siege to Leningrad, cutting off external supplies of nearly everything, including food. The Soviet government responded by implementing strict rationing and controlling food distribution. The citizens of Leningrad faced extreme hunger and starvation, as food became increasingly scarce.

The Khmer Rouge Regime in Cambodia: 1975-1979. In what is probably one of the most well-known examples of a government using food against its people, the Khmer Rouge regime, led by Pol Pot, forcefully relocated urban populations to rural areas and implemented socialist agricultural practices. The limited food produced by their harsh practices, untrained workers, and centralized control led to widespread famine. Millions of Cambodians died due to forced labor, executions, and starvation.

Chapter 8: Food Reality

Authoritarianism is always an option for those who sense their grip on power is slipping. To think that somehow "this time is different" would be foolish. The hyper efficiency of the global food supply chain has caused both natural and economic ecosystems to move outside of the window of viability. The world's governments are, therefore, positioning themselves to "take advantage of a good crisis."

In July 2022, *The Epoch Times* released a seventy-five-page magazine entitled *The Coming Food Crisis - And How to Prepare for It*.[52] It reveals that the United Nations and multinational corporations intend to squeeze out small farmers and capture control of the food supply (pg 8). It updated Kissinger's quote with one from Tom DeWeese, founder and chief of the American Policy Center. He understands the historical record and warns, "If people are starving, they are much easier to subjugate." (pg 14) The magazine also reveals China's growing influence in U.S. agricultural policy and its growing appetite for U.S. farmland. (pg 42) It discusses how the global food supply has become dependent on chemical fertilizers and the consequences of shortages and disruption. (pg 58).

When I first read the magazine, I wanted to believe it was alarmist. "Things are not that bad. (Are they?)" "Everything will be fine (Maybe? Hopefully?)" However, it became evident, after further research, that despite all that I have learned and written about, I too was tempted to allow naïve and ignorant thoughts to rationalize away historical and present reality. It's that powerful.

Summary

The last three chapters may have been unpleasant to read and consider. However, the liberty, security, and prosperity of God's people have always been tied directly and inseparably to the covenant between humanity, God, Jesus, and Creation. The sin of land defilement through bloodshed, unjust conquest, and idol worship has undermined that covenant throughout history. Today, the consequences are once again at our doorstep. Each year that passes without the ekklesia taking

---

[52] https://epochshop.com/products/special-edition-the-coming-food-crisis-75-page-magazine

decisive action to correct our economic and monetary injustices greatly increases our challenges to fulfill our Genesis 1:28 mission.

Today, there are countless initiatives worldwide in which people and organizations are combining environmental stewardship and local business investment to secure local food supply chains and strengthen their local economies. The people leading them understand the times.

And few of them are followers of Jesus.

In fact, further research reveals that many are aligned with groups hostile to God and His people. What does that mean for our communities in the years to come? Our families? Future generations? Please consider these questions carefully.

At the same time, as we face the monetary, economic, and food realities presented in these last chapters, we must not act out of fear of scarcity, economic collapse, or control by the systems designed by the kings of the earth. This is all happening because God is shining a light on the folly of the traditions of men. He is asking us to understand the times, know what to do, *and do it.*

It begins with cultivating and keeping the land God gave us to steward in our communities to help build a stable and sustainable food supply chain. Then, as the "Great Reset" and God's Great Restoration clash on the battlefield, the enemy cannot use food to control us or our neighbors. That brings us to Part 3, where I will propose steps that anyone can take to help build a critical mass of believers who will participate in the creation of new economic ecosystems in their communities.

Part 3
Covenant Restored

Chapter 9
Apply a New Economic Worldview

> "'For My thoughts are not your thoughts, Nor are your ways My ways,' declares the LORD. 'For as the heavens are higher than the earth, So are My ways higher than your ways And My thoughts than your thoughts.'"
> Isaiah 55:8-9

Movements that change lives on a large scale are driven by people who understand their "why?" They are motivated by an outcome they deeply desire for themselves, their families, and humanity in general. But the greatest determining factor that makes these people world changers is their anchor to a belief system—a worldview—that gives them the confidence to press forward in the face of extreme opposition. The movements reach critical mass when enough people begin to *apply* their worldview to their lives. This is true for all major cultural movements, whether secular or faith based.

It is arguable that over the last twenty years the kings of the earth have been more successful than the followers of Jesus at creating movements that change culture. There are several reasons for this.

1. They are passionately dedicated to their worldview and the outcomes they desire.
2. Their worldview is not bound by rules or ethics. For them, the means justify the ends.
3. They leverage influence over institutions to create an "anointed class" and hold them out as an unquestionable authority.
4. Those authorities create complex systems that manage major institutions such as law, government, health care, and economics.

5. Their media friends set the public narrative by using ambiguous and lofty terms, making it difficult to question the wisdom of the authorities and, thus, the systems and the outcomes they produce.

Much of their success comes from decades of "dumbing down" the population. For nearly two generations, the publicly controlled education system has left a large percentage of the population without the critical thinking and communication skills needed to penetrate the complexity/ambiguity matrix. Many who initially question the narrative find themselves faced with intense backlash and gaslighting that eventually wears them down.

It may surprise you to learn that the Pharisees used this very strategy in Jesus' day. They created a complex system of traditions that enabled them to confuse the Jewish people. Any who dared question these traditions were labeled heretics and "cancelled" from participating in "civil society."

This combination of political, religious, and narrative setting power resembled what many today call the "deep state." And like today, it functioned incredibly well—until Jesus came. He not only taught a new worldview but demonstrated how to *apply it* despite the tyranny of the Pharisee's traditions. A simple message of repent, love God, love your neighbor, and work together to build God's Kingdom shattered the Pharisees' system, and set the people free.

Today, we have the same opportunity. The current shaking of the world's systems has disrupted centuries of inertia. The complex economic and monetary traditions of men that have been thrust upon humanity by the kings of the earth are failing. Their replacement will either be a more complex set of systems imposed during a "Great Reset," or new systems designed according to common-sense biblical principles, during a "Great Restoration" of an age-old covenant. Given the worldview crisis that exists in today's church, restoring God's ways will be no small task.

The Covenant Throughout Scripture

Thus far, I have attempted to build a solid case from the early chapters of Genesis of a de facto covenant God initiated with humanity in the

Chapter 8: Food Reality

Garden of Eden. There are numerous accounts in Scripture that directly or indirectly validate the existence of this covenant. Let's take a moment and look closely at one of the most compelling.

The story of Joseph encompassed nearly one-third of the book of Genesis. Of the many important themes revealed through his life story, one is obvious and profound. Proper stewardship of Creation's abundant provision is critical to human survival. God placed Joseph in a position to preserve the nation of Israel through a severe famine, even though it ultimately led to 430 years of slavery in Egypt.

Then, to free Israel from bondage, God unleashed a series of plagues. The cumulative impact of each plague increasingly made it more difficult for the Egyptians to provide food for their families. Blood filled the water, killing fish and making it unsuitable for drinking. Frogs, lice, flies, disease, boils, hail, and locusts destroyed either animals or plants or both. Combined, these plagues had a direct and profound impact on the Egyptian food supply.

While there are many reasons Pharoh ultimately relented and let God's people go, I submit that a major contributing factor was the growing food supply crisis. Had similar plagues continued, Egypt would have faced another famine. Only this time, they did not have seven years to prepare for it, or a Joseph to lead them through it.

He who controls the food controls the decision-making process of people, including secular leaders. After God delivered the Israelites from Egypt, He told them that He was giving them a land "flowing with milk and honey." God intended to return them to a "garden" where the covenant to "cultivate and keep" the land could be re-established, and they would witness its ability to provide for them in abundance.

Sadly, they rejected God's offer. Therefore, He placed them in a land that was anything but flowing with milk and honey. In fact, they did not even have an opportunity to cultivate and keep a garden. Instead, the land was so barren that God had to provide them with manna for forty years.

Indeed, He who controls the food, controls the people.

The question before us today is, do we want God, working together with His people and applying His principles and ways, to control our food supply? Or do we want to leave control with today's Pharaohs?

In chapter three, I touched on the offerings made by Cain and Abel. I suggested that Adam and Eve had passed down rituals to remind their children of the need to cultivate and keep Creation and to express their gratitude for its ability to provide for them in abundance. These rituals were the precursor to the ceremonial offerings, feasts, and festivals in the Mosaic Law: Passover, the Feast of Unleavened Bread, the Feast of First Fruits, the Feast of Weeks, the Feast of Trumpets, and the Feast of Tabernacles.

Note that the prerequisite for each feast was the presence of abundant food. This is direct evidence that the covenantal relationships between God, His Son, Creation, and humans was intended as a centering point to provide for their physical, emotional, and spiritual well-being. The celebrations and feasts were His way to ensure we continually acknowledged the gift of Creation to provide abundant food for that purpose.

These accounts demonstrate the importance of the covenant from an Old Testament perspective. As we turn our focus to the New Testament, the first event that leaps off the pages is found in the narrative of Jesus' birth. Of all the people to whom God could have chosen to reveal the coming of the King, He chose the "lowly" shepherds. God highly valued these faithful keepers of the covenant and provided them with a front-row seat to one of the most important events in human history.

Fast forward to Jesus' ministry. After He was baptized and began His ministry, Jesus went into the wilderness and fasted. He was hungry. So, what did Satan do? He reverted to the strategy that was successful with Eve. His first attempt to get Jesus to sin was to invite him to "take" and use food for a purpose not intended by God. Of course, that attempt failed. However, it does demonstrate Satan's commitment to leverage what he accomplished in the Garden.

Now, let's briefly look at other instances when Jesus used food to make profound points in His ministry.

Chapter 8: Food Reality

- He told us not to worry about obtaining it.[53]
- He created it in abundance, as needed, and according to His will.[54]
- He used the people's understanding of the importance of food to draw them to an understanding of the importance of who *He* is.[55]
- At the end of His ministry, Jesus chose to spend the last evening prior to His death sharing a meal with those with whom He had formed His closest relationships.
- During that meal Jesus instituted the sacrament of communion. It symbolically, yet directly, tied the consumption of something brought forth by Creation—bread and wine—to His physical body and blood.

The point of listing these is to demonstrate the proliferation of the evidence that the Genesis covenant is real. Keeping it, or not keeping it, led to real consequences in the lives of God's people. For further evidence, I invite you to do a search in the entire Bible and simply read verses that contain the following seven words.

- Seed
- Food
- Bread
- Eat
- Abundance
- Steward/Stewardship
- Money

Armed with a fresh understanding of the Creation narrative and the examples above, many verses will now leap off the page, as you "see" them within a broader context of God's intended economy. They will open fresh revelation that you can apply to your life as they solidify the importance of the covenant as the foundation of an economic worldview that God always intended humanity to live by.

---

[53] Matthew 6:25
[54] Matthew 14:19
[55] John 4:32-38, 6:27, 6:55

Grounding yourself in a biblical economic worldview is so important that the sub-title of my second book, *My Ways*, is *A New Economic Worldview For the 21st Century Ekklesia*. Chapter six is entitled "Worldview Anchored." An extended excerpt is included here to lay a foundation that will help convey the importance of applying this new economic worldview in our families, churches, communities, and nations.

"Our response to such a crisis is to restore a comprehensive biblical worldview in the church. While this may seem obvious, the path to restoration is not. As radical as it may seem, I believe establishing a biblical *economic* worldview is a critical first step. Let me explain.

In the introduction, I made the case that economics is the network of rivers, lakes, and streams that direct the flow of life-giving resources to and between the so-called seven mountains of culture. The point was that economic systems touch everything. They harness the economic energy of God's people for the administration of God's work on earth.

Remember, the Greek word for "administration" is *oikonomia*, which means to steward resources for the benefit of the owner of a household. The Scripture at the beginning of this chapter, along with Ephesians 3:8-10, provides the ekklesia with an administrative and thus, an *economic* directive.

> "To me, the very least of all saints, this grace was given, to preach to the Gentiles the unfathomable riches of Christ, and to bring to light what is the administration of the mystery which for ages has been hidden in God who created all things; so that the manifold wisdom of God might now be made known through the church to the rulers and the authorities in the heavenly places."
> Ephesians 3:8-10

The life and teachings of Christ bring to light the mystery of God's will. The ekklesia can then make the manifold wisdom of God known to the rulers and authorities in heavenly places. Properly administering

Chapter 8: Food Reality

God's ways will lead to the fullness of times, when all things will be "summed up" in the heavens and earth in Christ.

Wow. What an incredible responsibility! As the ekklesia, we are given the privilege to co-labor with God and His council to design systems that will administer activities on earth in such a way that it will prepare us to receive our King. When we consider this, several questions regarding our present economic and monetary systems come to mind...

- Is it the manifold wisdom of God to acquire the resources to build His Kingdom by biting and devouring one another in the marketplace?

- Is it the manifold wisdom of God to use those resources to create for ourselves a level of comfort and affluence only enjoyed by kings a mere one-thousand years ago while our streets remain filled with poor, orphans, and widows?

- Is it the manifold wisdom of God that the ekklesia embraces economic and monetary systems created by the kings of the earth that historically and predictably fail, leaving a trail of hardship and suffering in their wake?

- Is it the manifold wisdom of God that the ekklesia embraces economic and monetary systems that lead to the rape and pillage of the earth's natural resources and destruction of the environment?

Of course, it is not. It is illogical, even absurd, to embrace systems that are designed by the very "rulers and authorities in the heavenly places" to whom we are supposed to make known *God's* manifold wisdom. Yet here we are. Large numbers of followers of Jesus are devoid of a general biblical worldview. Fewer still understand the economic principles by which God intended us to build His Kingdom. Until we correct this, the church will continue to harvest tares and the world's citizens will continue to suffer the consequences.

Embracing an Identity-Centered Worldview

Many followers of Jesus struggle to live according to a biblical worldview because they live in a world dominated by systems designed according to the basic principles of the world. The enemy uses these systems to chip away at each person's identity as an image bearer of God. Without even knowing it, people gradually embrace the traditions of men, and the Word of God loses its power in their lives.

Failure to understand what it means to be created "in the image of God"[56] is a major contributing factor to their struggles. Dr. Michael Heiser has carefully studied this critical matter, and He concludes that bearing God's "image" means to perform on earth a *role or accomplish an objective* that only He can do.[57]

As Dr. Heiser puts it, God created creatures like Him to be Him on earth to accomplish His will. Dr. Heiser uses the term "imagers" to convey this interpretation. We see this view supported by the Apostle Paul when he describes the combination of the divine and human nature of Jesus.

"He [Jesus] is the image of the invisible [spiritual] God, the firstborn of all creation."
Colossians 1:15

"For it was the Father's good pleasure for all the fullness to dwell in Him"
Colossians 1:19

"For in Him all the fullness of Deity [spiritual] dwells in [inside of a] bodily form,"
Colossians 2:9

These verses, and others like them, tell us that Jesus became God's full and perfect "imager" on earth.[58] His human body became the vessel through which the fullness of God's *objectives* manifest on the

---

[56] Genesis 1:26,27
[57] Dr. Michael Heiser, *The Unseen Realm*, Chapter 5
[58] John 14:7-11, 17:6

earth. The good news is that while we are partial and imperfect, we too are God's "imagers." That means we can assist in accomplishing God's objectives *only by bearing His image*—just as Jesus did. Multiple New Testament Scriptures are clear on this point.

> "and [we] have put on the new self who is being renewed to a true knowledge according to the image of the One who created him."
> Colossians 3:10

> "For those whom He foreknew, He also predestined to become conformed to the image of His Son..."
> Romans 8:29

> "...work out your salvation with fear and trembling; for it is God who is at work in you, both to will and to work for His good pleasure."
> Philippians 2:12-13

> "Therefore, we are ambassadors for Christ, as though God were making an appeal through us; we beg you on behalf of Christ, be reconciled to God. He made Him who knew no sin to be sin on our behalf so that we might become the righteousness of God in Him."
> 2 Corinthians 5:20-21

This last Scripture provides the context of all related verses listed before. The Greek word for "become" literally means to come into existence. As a believer in Jesus, you are created to manifest God's righteousness on earth by bearing His Son's image. As a perfect human imager, Jesus fully manifested God's role on earth by fully accomplishing the objectives assigned to Him. While we are imperfect imagers and, therefore, can manifest only a subset of God's objectives on earth, that is still quite a privilege!

An example of how our biological children "bear" our image may help explain how this works. Human children bear a subset of their parents' DNA in their physical bodies. They inherit a subset of their looks, health, and temperament. Their physical bodies are thus a subset of their parent's "image." This principle also applies to our spiritual identity as God's children, enabling us collectively to accomplish His ultimate objective – which is to build His Kingdom on earth![59]

Understanding this nuanced definition of our identity is essential. Satan knows the power we carry when, by bearing God's image, we accomplish even a tiny subset of His objectives on earth. It is why he enlisted the kings of the earth to create economic and monetary systems designed to use trading floors that seek to separate humans from their identities as God's image bearers. And it is why he jealously guards these systems.

Sadly, he continues to manage these systems with stunning success. He has so confused people about their identities, that many today, including a sitting United States Supreme Court Justice, cannot answer the question, "What is a woman?" Identity theft is so widespread that people now claim that men can menstruate and have babies. It is why they also believe elementary school-aged children should be allowed to choose their gender identity.

We should all be concerned when people who are so deceived about their identities sit in positions of authority in our government and schools. Reversing this process will take time. A primary reason I wrote *I Came to Give* and *My Ways* was to help bring *the economics of identity* into the biblical worldview discussion.

Success may seem an impossible task because few followers of Jesus understand the principles and spirits that drive socialism (control), capitalism (competition), and corporatism (the unholy alliance between the two). However, we have hope. For years, God has been revealing His economic principles to many, both inside and outside of the church, through "general revelation."

"For since the creation of the world His invisible attributes, His eternal power and divine nature, have been clearly seen,

---

[59] John 1:12

Chapter 8: Food Reality

being understood through what has been made, so that they are without excuse."
Romans 1:20

As mentioned in the last chapter, secular economists such as Bernard Lietaer and documentary filmmakers have glimpsed the beauty of God's ways. Therefore, I believe God will use these people to create a bridge for pastors who have been taken captive by secular philosophy to find their way back to the truth.

Eventually, economic instability will provide added motivation for these wayward pastors and their flocks to demand an answer to the question, "Why is this happening?" In his book *Discipling Nations*, Darrow Miller answers this question by pointing out that worldviews always determine economic outcomes.

Miller offers President Lyndon Johnson's "war on poverty" as an example. For over sixty years, the U.S. government spent tens of trillions of dollars on anti-poverty programs. Yet poverty remains a problem in the United States. In fact, due to present economic realities (2022), it is becoming worse. His explanation of why this is happening is sound:

"The fact is, different sets of ideas produce distinct behaviors, individually and corporately. These behaviors become institutionalized in the laws and structures of society, leading to poverty and other forms of brokenness.

[Poverty remains] because nothing was done to transform the worldview of the recipients.

Man's alienation from God (and disregard of God's principles) produces a mindset of poverty that further poisons the mind, spirit, and heart."[60]

He then rightfully notes:

"...truth sets people and nations free to thrive. It is safe to say that

---
[60] Darrow Miller, *Discipling Nations*, page 43

metaphysical capital is more important to flourishing than physical capital."[61]

Read that again. Metaphysical capital (spiritual well-being) is more important to human flourishing than physical capital (stuff). This may seem obvious, however, in the 21st Century economics of neo-Darwinian corporatism it is anything but.

Miller goes on to note that the church cannot expect to develop "metaphysical capital" (that is spiritual well-being) by simply giving a man a fish so that he has food for the day. He also notes that "development" programs, which teach a man to fish, so he has food for a lifetime, while better, are still not the answer. Miller makes the point that God's principles and ways of *how* to fish also matter! Adopting them is the only way cultures can be truly transformed, and that will only happen when a comprehensive biblical worldview permeates the culture.[62]

As Miller notes, "A worldview does more to influence people's flourishing—their prosperity or poverty—than does their physical environment or other circumstances."[63] This is the very reason why leaders and citizens of communities must embrace the five economic principles of cooperation, stewardship, abundance, identity, and sustainability as part of a comprehensive biblical worldview. It does not matter how radical they may seem. Bearing God's image and living according to His principles and ways are the only means to produce the outcomes He desires as the world enters a critical period of massive transformation."

(end excerpt)

God desires to change lives forever as people begin to live within the blessing of a new economic worldview. It really is no more complicated than that. So, as we transition from the "why" to the "how," I must highlight three key points.

---

[61] Ibid page 49
[62] Romans 12:2
[63] Darrow Miller, *Discipling Nations*, 12

Chapter 8: Food Reality

First, while economic shaking will indeed interrupt inertia, a tremendous amount of energy is required to set a new course. This is particularly true when "other forces" will use all the energy at their disposal to maintain their present economic dominance. Make no mistake. We are at war for the future economic destiny of nations. Achieving our desired outcomes will require a multi-step, multi-phase approach that will take years, if not a generation or more, to fully manifest.

Second, while it will take time, *we have the wind at our backs.* The awakening of the ekklesia is real. I have had recent conversations with people from many different nations and backgrounds. Some are interested in regenerative agriculture. Others are pastors of local churches. Still others lead national and international organizations. Their desire to restore stewardship of Creation as the foundation of local economic development has exceeded my expectations.

Additionally, there is a growing movement in which Christian organizations and individuals active in agriculture and community transformation and are seeking to join forces. It is exciting to see the Holy Spirit move in this area, and it should encourage us as we take steps to embrace and apply an economic biblical worldview in our households, churches, and communities.

As this movement gains momentum, we must remain clear-eyed and resolute. Practical implementation may happen during turbulent times. That means we must secure the home front first. Like flying on a commercial airliner, if there is a loss of cabin pressure, your responsibility is to put on your oxygen mask before you help others. The reason is simple. If you become incapacitated, you cannot help others. Instead, someone else must spend their time and energy helping you. That brings me to Paul's teaching in Galatians 6.

> "Let us not lose heart in doing good, for in due time we will reap if we do not grow weary. So then, while we have opportunity, let us do good to all people, and *especially to those who are of the household of the faith.*"
> Galatians 6:9-10 (emphasis mine)

Some Christians are uncomfortable with the fact that Paul told the ekklesia that its *first priority* is to care for fellow followers of Jesus along with the poor, widows, and orphans. Essentially, he told the church, "Put on your oxygen mask first so that you can help others." When it comes to reforming the church's economic worldview, putting on your mask begins by embracing fundamental economic realities.

- *Economics is ubiquitous.* I made this point in the second paragraph of the Introduction for a reason. Economics is everywhere all the time. No human being on the planet can escape it. The implications are far-reaching and are the reason that the ekklesia must exercise its governing authority over a system that is so critical to humanity.

- *A person's identity impacts economies.* A person who is secure in their identity as an image bearer of God will make different economic choices than one who is not. The ekklesia must design systems that will protect human identity so they can direct their economic activity toward building God's Kingdom and not that of the kings of the earth.

- *Economics is at the center of all relationships.* "Economic energy" is created and exchanged on "trading floors" every time two or more human beings interact. The energy may be in the form of goods, services, or money. It also may build or destroy a person's emotional, physical, or spiritual well-being. Because it is so vital to understand this, the next chapter is devoted exclusively to this subject.

- *Food is the foundation of all economic activity.* Without food, there are no people. Without people, there is no one to build the Kingdom. That reality is why it is so important to understand the covenant God instituted between Himself, His Son, humans, and Creation, and why the first purpose He identified for humanity was to "cultivate and keep" the Garden of Eden.

Chapter 8: Food Reality

Hopefully by now it is evident to you that God is very involved in this thing we call "economics." He connected it directly to His Creation, where it reveals His glory,[64] His power, and His nature.[65] Creation intimately touches everything God values through a relational covenant He instituted in the Garden of Eden. It is necessary to honor that covenant if Creation is to yield its strength and abundantly produce the fundamental resources that will bless humanity while we build the Kingdom of God on earth.

In the next chapter we will examine a critical component of every economic system that determines where the value of those resources is directed. The power it wields in both the natural and spiritual realms is enormous. When the ekklesia learns how to harness and unleash this power, it will change the world forever.

---

[64] Psalm 8:1, 19:1, 104:24-25, et. al.
[65] Romans 1:20, Job 12:7-10, Job 38

Chapter 10
Know Your Trading Floors

> "You shall have a full and just weight; you shall have a full and just measure, that your days may be prolonged in the land which the LORD your God gives you."
> Deuteronomy 25:15

Economic systems build kingdoms. There is no escaping that practical reality. In the context of a biblical worldview, there are only two kingdoms that will be built by the fruit of a person's labor—the Kingdom of God or the kingdom of man. This explains why the spiritual war to gather resources to build those kingdoms is so intense. Any advantage one kingdom can gain over the other is critical. It also explains why, from the moment he encountered Eve in the garden, Satan used his skills in trade to create economic systems to steal, kill, and destroy the natural and spiritual resources created by God's people.

And all of this takes place on trading floors.

For our purposes, we define trading floors as the place where human beings exchange value. The exchange may involve goods, services, money, or non-tangible "items" that impact a person's emotional, physical, or spiritual well-being.

The concept of a trading floor is easy to grasp when you think of it in the context of a standard commercial transaction. You walk into a store, pick something off a shelf, take it to a cashier, and exchange money for the selected item. Value was exchanged, and trade occurred. Simple enough, right? Well, yes. However, there is much more happening in this "simple" trade when you examine it through a biblical economic worldview.

Before making any trade, we must first establish whether it is legal according to God's laws, not man's laws. The legal question is important because it directly relates to the *legitimacy of the trade*. This carries massive implications in the spiritual world and in the Kingdom of God. The following will give you a grid through which to grasp those implications.

Legal trades are binding. Illegal trades are illegitimate and can be reversed in a court with the proper jurisdiction. I will have more to say about this in the next chapter. For now, know that we can analyze trades from a biblical perspective to determine their legality by applying five basic rules.

Rule #1: The trade must be conducted according to a legitimate source of binding law. (jurisdictional authority)

Rule #2: The participants in the trade must have the right to offer and receive the item being traded. (legal stewardship)

Rule #3: The participants in the trade must understand and agree to the terms of the trade. (informed consent)

Rule #4: The participants in the trade must not be under duress or subject to any unfair disadvantage in negotiations. (equal bargaining power)

Rule #5: After the trade, the item traded will become an asset for the kingdom that the receiving party is building. (contract fulfillment)

Most people have a general sense of these legal principles. For followers of Jesus, our point of reference for defining the rules of the trade is not man's law but the principles and covenants God established to build His Kingdom. Unfortunately, this is where the ekklesia has failed to understand the power of the trading floor.

Before we continue, we need to take a moment to address a legal principle that is critical to our discussion. *Stare decisis*. The Cornell Law School defines it as follows.

> "Stare decisis is the doctrine that courts will adhere to precedent in making their decisions. Stare decisis means "to stand by things decided" in Latin. When a court faces a legal

Chapter 10: Know Your Trading Floors

argument, if a previous court has ruled on the same or a closely related issue, then the court will make their decision in alignment with the previous court's decision."[66]

This important principle directly involves rule #1, which identifies the legitimate source of binding law. Now, this may seem obvious, but for followers of Jesus, *in the jurisdiction of the Kingdom of God, His Word is the only legitimate foundation for "all things decided."* Any law, principle, or precedent not in alignment with what He established "in the beginning" is illegitimate and non-binding in the Kingdom of God. It matters not whether the kings of the earth, or any other authority delegated by them, write laws to the contrary.

When examining trade laws, applying *stare decisis* requires us to return to the original source and determine the original intent of the law-giving body. For followers of Jesus, the law-giving body is God. The text of the law is the Bible. Regarding economics, that takes us back to John 1:1-5 and Genesis 1 and 2. This is where God established His covenant (binding law) with humanity and revealed the principles that enable us to honor that covenant.

The first five chapters of *My Ways* draw a stark contrast between the principles God established as legal precedent for His economic system and those that Satan offers as an alternative. Unfortunately, as you know, Satan's illegitimate principles have been used for centuries to codify economic and monetary law and thus dominate the rules of today's trading floors. For brevity's sake, I will provide a summary of the conclusions of each of the five chapters so you can see the contrast.

- Chapter 1: Cooperation vs control and competition. A trading floor based on the principles of control and competition is inward-focused and puts the parties in the trade at odds with one another. These principles incentivize each party to maximize their benefit at the expense of the other. It leaves little room for additional value to be created during the trade. A trading floor based on cooperation is outward-focused. The parties understand that working together can create much more value in the trade. Ultimately, this accrues greater benefit

---

[66] https://www.law.cornell.edu/wex/stare_decisis

to all parties involved, as well as those outside the immediate trade (for example, their families or communities).

- Chapter 2: Stewardship vs ownership. A trading floor based on ownership is inward-focused. It results from the spirits of control and competition, creating the mindset that the *self* should be the primary beneficiary of the trade. A trading floor based on stewardship is outward-focused. Those conducting trade on it understand the primary beneficiary must be the Kingdom of God.

- Chapter 3: Abundance vs scarcity. A trading floor based on a scarcity mindset is inward-focused. Those conducting trade on it will attempt to tilt the outcome of the trade in their favor and obtain control over the most resources possible. A trading floor based on an abundance mindset is outward-focused. Those conducting trade on it understand that sufficient resources are available for all parties to benefit and additional value can be created.

- Chapter 4: Identity. *All* trading floors impact the identity of the parties in the trade. They will either encourage a person to embrace their identity as an image bearer of God, or to deny their identity and thus become a "spiritual orphan." These spiritual orphans are then vulnerable to "identity theft" as Satan recruits them to bear his image and join him in stealing, killing, and destroying assets meant for the Kingdom of God.

- Chapter 5: Sustainability vs efficiency. Trading floors that seek to maximize short-term gain increasingly move toward hyper-efficiency. They become fragile and vulnerable to single points of failure. A trading floor designed with sustainability in mind may consider short-term outcomes. However, its primary objective is to preserve a positive, generational impact on humanity, Creation, and the Kingdom of God.

Today's marketplace trading floors are based on man's principles. Even though they are illegitimate in the eyes of God, followers of Jesus

Chapter 10: Know Your Trading Floors

are bound, at least to some degree, by their rules because they are deeply embedded into life and culture. This has enabled the enemies of God to steal vast amounts of resources over countless generations. It is the direct result of God's people not taking their place in the design of economic systems according to God's Word, thereby establishing *His ways* as the basis for "all things decided."

The good news is that you have the power to set some of the rules by which your trades are conducted—even within economic systems designed by the kings of the earth. To do so, you must understand all of the value exchanged on your trading floors.

Today, schools and Universities only teach us the *transactional* nature of value exchange. They narrowly focus on the exchange of money, or at a minimum, some form of barter. However, monetary-based transactional trades are only a small contribution to God's economy. His economy involves much more than tangible goods and services. To understand this better, let's examine three categories of trading floors.

Your internal trading floor. Every waking moment, this floor is open. It consists of your thought life and the worldview you apply to the choices you make. You must manage it carefully. How you think about *everything* matters. Satan prefers that you remain unaware of the existence of this trading floor. He goes to great lengths to distract you from understanding its presence and power. In his book, *The Life We're Looking for: Reclaiming Relationship in a Technological World*, Andy Crouch describes perfectly one of Satan's strategies to manage this trading floor for us.[67]

> "Our minds drift and wander, seeking comfort and familiarity rather than challenge and creativity. Our strength atrophies-how many of us can say that we maintain a healthy pattern of exertion and fatigue, work, and rest? Instead, we fall into vicious cycles of inactivity and lethargy... The honest truth is that often, we just give in. We make choices that accelerate the patterns of emptiness and loneliness rather than reverse them."

---

[67] Andy Crouch, *The Life We're Looking For*, pg 35-36

The thoughts, images, and sounds we allow into our lives constantly strengthen or weaken us emotionally and spiritually. They affirm our identity as image bearers of God, or they deny it. They either increase the quality of our relationship with God and His Creation or decrease it. Increase or decrease. That can only happen as the result of a trade.

God's enemies understand this much better than we do. If they can distract people from intentionally managing this trading floor, they will. Their goal is to weaken their target's identity in Christ. Eventually, lethargy and apathy will cause them to cast aside a biblical worldview, making their trades neutral at best. At worst, the target will become an agent who willingly, or unwillingly, gathers resources for Satan's kingdom.

This process is step one in Satan's economic strategy to gather the resources needed to displace God's Kingdom on earth and "be like the Most High."[68]

We see this strategy in action in the documentary *The Century of the Self*, and in the book *The Rise and Triumph of the Modern Self*. It is imperative that you fully understand that your identity determines which kingdom your value will build. God wants you to steward that value to benefit His Kingdom, you, and your loved ones. In that order. Satan wants you to deploy that value for the benefit of his kingdom first, and that happens when you claim it as yours (ownership) and seek to primarily benefit yourself (scarcity). When followers of Jesus grasp this, the ekklesia will gain the worldview clarity necessary to create and manage two additional types of trading floors based on God's principles.

Relational trading floors. While your internal trading floor impacts how you maintain your identity, and thus how you steward your resources, relational trading floors directly impact the identity of others. A familiar passage in the book of James lays the foundation for understanding the power of these trading floors.

---

[68] Isaiah 14:13,14

Chapter 10: Know Your Trading Floors

"But no one can tame the tongue; it is a restless evil and full of deadly poison. With it we bless our Lord and Father, and with it we curse men, who have been made in the likeness of God; from the same mouth come both blessing and cursing."
James 3:8-10a

With our tongue, we can bless or curse our fellow image bearers. The result is to either increase or decrease their emotional and/or spiritual well-being. *Increase or decrease.* Again, this can only occur during a trade. James identified the asset in the trade—those "who have been made in the likeness of God." This passage is one of several in Scripture that point to the identity of human beings as the center of spiritual warfare, *subject to change based on how we conduct trade within our economic systems.*

Man's economic systems want everything to be transactional. God wants them to be relational. Until followers of Jesus intentionally bring the relational value into all our trading floors, especially those designed by man, the enemies of God will continue to make progress in thwarting the advancement of God's Kingdom.

How do we do that? Consider that billions of people worldwide engage in trade each day through the mere act of having a conversation. No money is exchanged. Yet depending on how the tongue is used, each person's identity is impacted, for good or ill. That means each time we speak with our fellow human beings, *the Kingdom of God or the kingdom of darkness gains from the trade that occurs on the relational trading floor.*

These trades have been occurring since Adam and Eve were placed in the Garden of Eden. When Satan engaged in his conversation with Eve, little did she know that he brought her onto a relational trading floor. Let's take a moment and deconstruct what happened in that encounter and the resulting consequences.

1) Using his tongue, Satan drew Eve onto relational and marketplace (see below) trading floors.
2) Neither Satan nor Eve was given stewardship of the items in the trade. For Satan it was Eve. For Eve, the fruit. Thus, any outcome is fraudulent and thus illegitimate in God's eyes.

3) Satan's mere words caused Eve to exchange the truth for a lie, become a thief, defile Creation, and break the covenant.
4) At that moment, she took up and bore an impostor's image and her identity as a bearer of *only* God's image, ended.

What took place in the Garden was a tragedy of epic proportions. Satan's trading floors broke all five rules of legitimate trade. Yet, through that one trade, he set an illegitimate precedent as *stare decisis,* and man has used it to design economic systems throughout history with trading floors based on control, competition, scarcity, identity theft, and efficiency.

This, my friend, is the power of trading floors. The mere act of initiating a conversation with another human being can result in consequences far beyond producing tangible or monetary resources to build kingdoms. The value of a person's very identity as God's image bearer is at stake. Ultimately, how we impact their identity can shape not only the trades *they* make, but future generations—either for good or for ill. Followers of Jesus should beg God for the awareness and discernment to understand the power of these critical relational trading floors and manage them accordingly.

Marketplace trading floors. After considering our internal and relational trading floors, marketplace transactions may seem trivial. I assure you they are not. While many, if not most, of these trades are made with people we do not know personally, their impact on the Kingdom of God is substantial. An excerpt from *I Came to Give*, chapter ten, entitled, "Economics, Money, and the Kingdom of God," will demonstrate why.

"Let's look at a real-world example of how this works.

- Mr. and Mrs. Smith love Jesus. They each receive a $5,000 bonus.
- Mr. and Mrs. Smith put that money in their checking account.
- While in their account, it has the *potential* to be used to advance God's Kingdom. If they steward it according to our Kingdom building mandate, it will.

Chapter 10: Know Your Trading Floors

- Mr. and Mrs. Smith need a car. They do their research and find two cars they like. Both will cost about $10,000.
- Mr. and Mrs. Smith know the owners of both car dealers. One is a loyal Kingdom-minded person. The other is noted for less-than-ethical behavior.

Here are two possible scenarios that can play out:

1. Mr. and Mrs. Smith buy the car from the person they know loves Jesus. That person takes the profit of $1,000 and gives it to a local non-profit that just saved a child from a sex-trafficking ring in their community. The "economic energy" contained in the monetary items restored a human asset that will build the Kingdom of God.
2. Mr. and Mrs. Smith buy the car from the second person who uses the $1,000 profit to buy drugs from a contact at the corner gas station. The contact then takes the money and, two hours later, buys the child who would have been rescued, for sex. The "economic energy" contained in the monetary items went toward destroying two lives. This, of course, builds a very different kingdom.

Yes, this seems to be an extreme example. However, trades like these happen every day. We make choices to steward economic energy to advance the Kingdom of God or transfer it into the domain of the enemy. All too often we do not consider the flow-on effect of our choices. Yet the thief has *designed* today's economic and monetary systems to steal our economic energy and transfer it *out* of the domain of God's Kingdom at a *much greater rate than it flows in*. That is why we must ask some critical yet straightforward questions when choosing who we *trade* with:

- Are their values aligned with mine?
- What unintended consequences may result from this trade if the economic energy that I give them is deployed in opposition to God?

In a world as interconnected as ours, it is impossible to enter trading floors that keep *all* the economic energy we trade from falling into the wrong hands. However, we can slow the transfer of economic energy to those who oppose God's Kingdom by minding our marketplace trading floors and making wise and intentional choices. This is an important step for the church to restore a biblical economic worldview."

(end excerpt)

It really is no more complicated than that. Today, the enemies of God are aggressively gathering and deploying the resources generated on the world's marketplace trading floors in a deliberate effort to undermine the Kingdom of God. More than ever, you must carefully choose who you bring onto your trading floors. When it is in your power, define the rules of the trade to minimize the theft of your resources so that you maximize those available to deploy in the Kingdom of God. My prayer is that, based on what you learn in this chapter, you will now see, and more intentionally manage, each of your trading floors. However, we are not finished yet.

Micro Deposits

I want to leave the subject of trading floors by bringing to your attention one of the most powerful sources of value that followers of Jesus have at their disposal. Secular economic analysts focus on the trillions of dollars in global commercial trade conducted on marketplace trading floors each year. Yet their value pales in comparison to the value created and traded on relational and internal trading floors.

The primary reason is that the currency used on relational and internal trading floors is very different. It is not dollars, euros, yuan, pesos, or any other form of money designed by man's monetary systems to remain scarce. Instead, these trades are conducted in a currency that is unlimited in supply. And yes, in this case, that is a very good thing.

Earlier, we looked at the power of the tongue to increase or decrease human identity as image bearers of God. Increasing the

Chapter 10: Know Your Trading Floors

"balance" of that account occurs when we use our tongue to make "micro-deposits" of blessing while on a relational trading floor. These deposits can be in the form of a simple word of encouragement. They can be a smile given to a cashier who is having a tough day or treating other drivers on the road kindly. They can be comforting words given to a child who scraped a knee on the pavement, or a prayer given on a street corner to a homeless person.

It is hard to overstate the power of these micro-deposits. We live in a world where Satan works 24/7 to undermine people's emotional, physical, and spiritual well-being. Today, his goal is to use *us* to decrease a person's "identity as an image bearer of God" by speaking his currency of curses. He would like nothing more than use us to make people "spiritual orphans" that he can recruit to build his kingdom.

Understanding this, our choice to make micro-deposits of blessing is a front-line defense against this strategy. These deposits are a form of seed. Instead of being sown in the soil, they are sown in the souls of those we encounter daily. Seemingly small and insignificant, they hold the power to grow into something that will produce in abundance for generations—a life empowered to unleash the image of God that resides within every human being.

When followers of Jesus understand the power of unleashing micro-deposits of blessing on relational trading floors, it will change families and communities. When enough of us generously spend that currency, it has the potential to be nothing short of a tactical nuclear bomb in the spirit world. It will forever dislodge the iron grip that principalities and powers hold in every geographic territory where we make these micro-deposits in massive numbers. Satan's ability to conduct identity theft will be cut off, crippling forever his recruiting pipeline.

As this chapter comes to a close, take a moment and imagine a world where followers of Jesus intentionally manage their trading floors based on the *legitimate* precedent of stare decisis established by God in the Garden.

- Imagine that, over the next decade, your community begins to experience the cumulative impact of making micro-deposits of blessings into the emotional, physical, and spiritual "accounts" of your neighbors.

- Imagine that your community adopts an entirely new system of value creation and management that makes these deposits a more natural part of everyday life.

- Imagine local businesses working together to prioritize the creation of resources to secure and protect family and community identity, instead of maximizing profits and market share.

- Imagine churches in your community working together to build a sustainable local economic system that provides a pathway to dignity for the poor, orphans, and widows.

- Imagine a restored sense of awe and wonder for Creation and a commitment by your community to steward its resources for their highest and best use as the foundation for this new system.

- Now, imagine this happening in hundreds of thousands of communities around the world. Human beings find themselves on new trading floors where emotional scars and physical ailments are healed. They will then be set free to fully manifest the image of God within them to build His Kingdom on earth.

As untold millions of human beings exchange the lie (their identity as image bearers of the impostor) for the truth (their identity as God's image bearers), the Great Restoration of God's principles and ways will spread throughout the earth. And as the kings of the earth rage at the futility of their Great Reset to stop it, God will sit in the heavens and laugh.[69]

This, dear ekklesia, is the power of God's economic principles and ways, and it begins with understanding and managing our trading floors.

---

[69] Psalm 2

Chapter 11
Redeem the Land

"He said, "What have you done? The voice of your brother's blood is crying to Me from the ground. Now you are cursed from the ground, which has opened its mouth to receive your brother's blood from your hand. When you cultivate the ground, it will no longer yield its strength to you; you will be a vagrant and a wanderer on the earth.""
Genesis 4:10-12

To move our local economies back within the window of viability we must embrace an economic worldview that is aligned with God's principles and His ways. We must understand the impact that trading floors have on the creation, stewardship, and deployment of the many types of value that build His Kingdom. Yet a necessary key to restoring the foundational covenant God made in Genesis 1 and 2 is almost entirely overlooked by the body of Christ.

In chapter three, we discussed Satan's strategy to maximize the negative impact of sin on both humanity and Creation when Eve became a thief by stealing the fruit of the tree of knowledge of good and evil. It worked so well that he repeated his strategy in the next generation. Scripture says that when Cain shed Abel's innocent blood, it caused the land to "no longer yield its strength."[70]

Consider what that means in practical terms. God always intended the "strength" of the land to be its ability to produce abundant food and other natural resources. Not only for human beings, but for every creeping, crawling, walking, and swimming creature on earth, many

---

[70] Genesis 4:12

of which themselves are given to us as food.[71] Acts, such as shedding innocent human blood on the land, causes the land to produce much less than it is capable of.

In his book, *The Unseen Realm, Chapter 15 – Cosmic Geography*, Dr. Michael Heiser sets important context for how we can restore the "strength" of the land. First, he lays the foundation of territorial oversite of the land by *elohim* (little "g" gods) by examining passages such as Genesis 11:1-9 (the Tower of Babel), Daniel 10:13 (the prince of Persia), and:

> "When the Most High gave to the nations their inheritance,
> when he divided mankind, he fixed the borders of the
> peoples according to the number of the sons of God."
> Deuteronomy 32:8-9 (ESV)

Dr. Heiser demonstrates that, when the above verses are examined in their proper context, Paul alludes to them in Ephesians 6:12, 1 Corinthians 2:6,8, and Ephesians 3:10 when using terms such as "authorities," "rulers," "princes," "principalities," "powers," "dominions" and "thrones." He concludes, "These terms have something in common— they were used in both the New Testament and other Greek literature for *geographical domain rulership.*"

This is important to understand because when these "principalities and powers" drove humanity to shed innocent blood on the land (as was the case with Cain and Able) it defiled the land, limiting its ability to "give up its strength." The result was the imposition of satanic economic sanctions on the land.

Satanic economic sanctions.

Severely limiting Creation's ability to yield its strength has direct and profound economic consequences for the Kingdom of God. The trading floors the enemy created to defile the land and impose these sanctions go well beyond facilitating the spilling of innocent blood. Land acquired by unjust war, fraud, and cultural genocide against indigenous peoples is common to nearly every nation on earth. The resulting spiritual defilement enables the principalities and powers

---

[71] Genesis 1:29-30

Chapter 11: Redeem the Land

asserting geographical domain rulership to wreak havoc upon the citizens who inhabit the territory.

Reversing these fraudulent and illegal trades will achieve two important objectives. First, it will free the land to produce as intended—assuming the land then is properly stewarded. Second, it will revoke the authority of the "rulership" to harass the citizens inhabiting the land. The enemy knows this. Therefore, his "princes," "powers," and "rulers and authorities in the heavenly places" will jealously guard the land to maintain the impact of the defilements.

What I am about to say next is critical. God owns the land and everything in it.[72] He, and He alone, has the jurisdictional authority to lift the burden of defilements from the land.[73] Attempting to confront the "rulers" of the land by yourself can and will result in catastrophic consequences.

Richard and Kimberly Wilson, founders of Watchmen Arise, offer training for those who are serious about redeeming the land with care and wisdom. With their permission, I have woven some of their insights into the remainder of this chapter. It begins with understanding...

The Impact of Defilements

Protecting our identity as God's image bearer is one of the five economic principles upon which His Kingdom will be built. In the last chapter, we covered how managing our trading floors helps us do this for ourselves and others. We return again to Genesis 3 as we continue to glean from the richness of this all-important early text.

When Eve reached out and took control of a forbidden piece of God's Creation, it defiled both Creation and humanity. Satan's encounter with Adam and Eve thus corrupted human identity by co-mingling his image (willfully through sin) with theirs. Since then, God's image bearers unintentionally create defilements in the land when they succumb to the sin that results from this co-mingling.

Satan knows that as humans gain access to more territory, whether they bless or defile the land depends on the identity they bear when

---

[72] Leviticus 25:23, Psalm 50:10-12
[73] Genesis 6-8

they acquire it, and then how they steward it. It can either be acquired on protected trading floors and then stewarded according to the principles of the covenant, or it can be acquired through illegal trade on his trading floors which are laced with disobedience, deceit, or bloodshed.

My friends, our enemy understands this game to a degree few followers of Jesus do. He knows that land defilement begins in a household with a father and mother. He began his defilement campaign with Adam and Eve and their sons Cain and Abel. Left unchecked, it spread across time and culture, ultimately leading to the defilement of the entire earth. The Wilsons teach us how the depth of corruption of both humanity and Creation occurred, leading to the events of Genesis 6-8.

Before considering how to partner with God to remove land defilements, it is necessary to understand the nature of the iniquity that defiled the land that you are seeking to set free. That requires time, patience, research, and much prayer. Once you understand the spiritual "lay of the land," you can ask God how *He* wants to adjudicate it in *His* courts, according to stare decisis set by *His* principles.

The Wilsons help us in this process by identifying four primary categories of defilements. Each is designed by Satan to enable his satanic economic sanctions to remain in place for generations.

Idolatry

In His Word, God repeatedly warned the Israelites of the profound and lasting dangers of idolatry. I covered this extensively in chapter nine of *I Came to Give*. Therefore, I will begin this section with an excerpt from the section entitled "The Law."

"...[a] central theme of the meta-narrative of Deuteronomy is the importance of the nation of Israel maintaining its identity.

The way God chose to make this evident is highly instructive. Chapter four begins with a specific and urgent exhortation: Remember My statutes! Do not add to them or take away from them! Do not forget all that you have seen and all that I have done for you! Remember the Ten Commandments![74]

---

[74] Deuteronomy 4:1-14

Chapter 11: Redeem the Land

The remainder of chapter four focuses almost exclusively on *the first three commandments*. Remember, I am the One true God. There are no others. You are entering into a land that has worshiped false gods, idols, and images of all kinds for generations. I plead with you, do not worship them! Knowing they would fail,[75] God assures them that He will be there when they seek repentance.

Chapter four sets a pattern that continues through the following *eight* chapters. God continually urges them to follow His statutes and warnings about idol worship. All told, *over 30% of the book of Deuteronomy focuses on driving home the importance of keeping the first three commandments*. The generational blessings of obedience and the generational curses of disobedience are the consequences of success or failure. God makes His disdain for false images clear because of who they represent and what they do to His people.

> "The graven images of their gods you are to burn with fire; you shall not covet the silver or the gold that is on them, nor take it for yourselves, or you will be snared by it, for it is an abomination to the LORD your God. You shall not bring an abomination into your house, and like it come under the ban; you shall utterly detest it, and you shall utterly abhor it, for it is something banned."
> Deuteronomy 7:25-26

This passage flows directly into chapter eight, which contains essential lessons on the stewardship of God's provision. God reminds Israel that they were tested in the desert so that they would not forget that He will provide for their basic needs, and when it comes down to it, that, and His Word, are enough.[76]

God reminds them of this truth because He is about to give them a land that will yield an enormous increase in resources. They will need to steward these resources according to His principles to enjoy the abundance and growth He desires for them.[77]

Then comes a stern warning. Beware! There is danger. The hearts of the people will become inclined to believe *they* were the ones who

---

[75] Deuteronomy 4:25-31
[76] Deuteronomy 8:1-5
[77] Deuteronomy 8:6-10

gained the power to create material wealth from these abundant natural resources. They will become proud of "their accomplishments" and forget that God owns everything and is the only source from which their increase flows.[78]

God is fulfilling His covenant to provide a way for His image bearers to preserve the principles that will enable humanity to fulfill their mandate to build His Kingdom on earth. He did not prosper His people so they could live a life of comfort and ease. Imagers living only for this purpose bear God's name in vain. They misrepresent to the world who He is, what He values, and what He created human beings to accomplish.[79]

> "But you shall remember the LORD your God, for it is He who is giving you power to make wealth, *that He may confirm His covenant which He swore to your fathers, as it is this day.*"
> Deuteronomy 8:18 (emphasis mine)

In the verses just before this passage, God said that material abundance would *lead to their undoing*. Therefore, taken in the proper context, it is evident that the wealth God refers to here is *not* gold, silver, and large flocks. Instead, cultivating (serving) Creation and stewarding its abundant resources will produce a "wealth" of emotionally, physically, and spiritually healthy human imagers that would "be fruitful and multiply." Only then can they fulfill their purpose and advance the Grand Building Project [Build God's Kingdom on earth].

(end excerpt)

Idolatry begins when the enemy draws a person onto a trading floor and a portion of their identity as God's image bearer is exchanged for that of the impostor. When compromised by idolatry, the principalities and powers occupying the defiled land influence the person's motives and drive them to make choices that advance the kingdom of darkness.

A significant step toward dealing with idolatry begins when a person redeems a piece of land and stewards it according to the terms

---

[78] Deuteronomy 8:11-17
[79] Deuteronomy 8:18-19

of the covenant. It could be no more than a cup of dirt. By planting a bean or a few herbs and putting it on a windowsill, one will witness the wonder of Creation producing life-giving food. This could be the opening that spiritually reconnects that person to the Creator as they cultivate and keep their tiny garden.

Immorality

The second category of defilements identified by the Wilsons was also manifested in the Garden of Eden. Immorality is the natural progression that occurs when idolatry goes unchecked. This can manifest in a community when a critical mass of people takes on the character and nature of God's enemies and idolatry and immorality become embedded in the culture.

The evidence of land defilement often begins with unjust domination/control over fellow human beings (i.e. Adam's domination over Eve). Soon, it is no longer confined to private homes and isolated acts of violence against families and neighbors. It spills into the streets and spreads like cancer on the earth. Today, there is evidence of this occurring in cities all over the world.

- Sexual perversions are normalized. Humans are made into sex slaves, sold to the highest bidder to satisfy the lusts of the flesh.

- Humans created in the image of God are dehumanized and destroyed through acts of abortion and "voluntary" euthanasia.

- Racism and prejudice are used as a wedge to create division rather than working toward reconciliation and cooperation.

- Depression, anxiety, self-esteem, shame, and suicidal thoughts become commonplace and nearly normalized.

Today, we see immorality's contribution to land defilements worldwide. For decades we have been sliding into the abyss described in the first chapter of Romans, to the point of experiencing the wrath of God described in the second chapter. This is the tenuous position we find ourselves in today.

Bloodshed and Broken Covenants

Recall that Cain's murder of Abel was the origin of bloodshed as a land defilement. It was, and remains, a primary stronghold that empowers the enemies of God on earth today. That is because God takes covenantal relationships seriously,[80] and thus violating the original covenant to serve and protect the land set in motion a dangerous pattern.

We see it in the historical record which is filled with broken covenants that impact the land. Just as a single example, we know that the United States government broke hundreds of covenants with Native Americans. The bloodshed and resulting defilements impacted the land's ability to "yield its strength" across the nation.

Our response has not been to repent, but instead, to take matters into our own hands. We have applied our wisdom to land ownership and turned natural ecosystems into man-made chemical plots where GMO grains produce tremendous yields that we arrogantly label as "yielding its strength." All the while we have sacrificed sustainability and the land's true strength – the ability to produce nutrient rich foods that God designed to keep our bodies healthy.

As a result, citizens of the United States have become some of the unhealthiest in the world. In the 1960s, chronic disease was studied as an anomaly. Today, the multi-billion-dollar pharmaceutical industry manages (and profits heavily from) the 60% plus of the population that suffers from them.

These are the cumulative consequences of millennia of broken covenants and land defilements that have not been recognized or repented of by God's people. The Wilsons connect a key Scripture to these consequences that should have us crying out to God for mercy.

> "The earth mourns and withers, the world fades and withers, the exalted of the people of the earth fade away. The earth is also polluted by its inhabitants, for they transgressed laws, violated statutes, broke the everlasting covenant. Therefore, a

---

[80] Psalms 25:14, 103:17-18

Chapter 11: Redeem the Land

curse devours the earth, and those who live in it are held guilty. Therefore, the inhabitants of the earth are burned, and few men are left."
Isaiah 24:4-6

Their description of this passage is sobering.

"Note the words: defiled, curse, and the statement "few men left": The earth mourns and fades away, The world languishes and fades away; The haughty people of the earth languish. The earth is also defiled under its inhabitants, Because they have transgressed the laws, Changed the ordinance, Broken the everlasting/eternal covenant. Therefore the curse has devoured the earth, And those who dwell in it are desolate. Therefore the inhabitants of the earth are burned, And few men are left."

Scholars do not agree about what the "everlasting covenant" is. Therefore, let's take a moment and examine the context of the proceeding verses for possible clues.

"Behold, the LORD lays the earth waste, devastates it, distorts its surface and scatters its inhabitants. And the people will be like the priest, the servant like his master, the maid like her mistress, the buyer like the seller, the lender like the borrower, the creditor like the debtor. The earth will be completely laid waste and completely despoiled, for the LORD has spoken this word." Isaiah 24:1-3

It is worth noting that the Hebrew word for "earth" used here is "eres" which directly references the created earth vs. "cosmos" which can include the earth's secular, man-made systems. The imagery here reminds us of the conditions in Genesis 6 that led to the events in chapters eight and nine. In chapter four of this book, I noted that during Noah's day, the bloodshed of the land was so great that it required the cleansing of both humanity and the created earth.

That judgment came about, at least in part, because humanity broke the covenant to cultivate and keep Creation. Note the phrases used by Isaiah in this passage, "polluted by its inhabitants," "transgressed laws," "violated statutes," "distorts its surface," and "laid waste." They paint a picture of an earth once again destroyed by man's failure to serve and protect Creation. So, I ask...

Could the "everlasting covenant" referred to here be the one described in the Creation narrative?

I do not claim this as a settled doctrine. However, in the context of the whole council of Scripture, it makes sense to consider it. God never changes. He consistently applies justice where the consequences fit the transgression. It is well established that one of the enemy's primary methods of operation is to force the land to give up its strength through broken covenants. If cultivating and keeping Creation is the "everlasting covenant," our global disregard for it would explain a great deal about why the world is in the state it is today.

Wisdom and Jurisdictional Boundaries

As we consider the impact of land defilements on our homes, communities, and nations, the Wilsons offer a word of caution. Tremendous wisdom is required when considering how to dislodge land defilements and lift the accompanying satanic economic sanctions. The principalities and powers associated with them are deeply embedded spiritually in the territory which they occupy. Most are multi-generational and touch defilements that are decades or centuries old.

That does not mean we should shy away from engaging them. However, as I stated earlier, we must honor God's jurisdictional authority over Creation and engage when *He clearly delegates* a measure of that authority to us for the specific purpose of cleansing the land. As a general rule, God will call you to partner with Him to displace principalities and heal the land where you have established a measure of natural jurisdictional authority. This generally includes the land He has entrusted to you to steward or land you occupy through your presence in a geographic location. For most, it will begin with your home. You may live in a rented apartment, own a house in the suburbs, or raise crops and livestock on a thousand-acre farm. *That* is the territory God has given you to steward, and that is the proper place to begin.

Chapter 11: Redeem the Land

Regardless of the size of the land that God has called you to steward, Richard and Kimberly Wilson's course on land redemption can provide you with the insight needed to align with God's strategy to deal with any defilements that may be present. It will also prepare you if He calls you to a larger assignment, such as dealing with defilements in your community or nation.

With that said, I am fully aware that the subject of land defilements and redemption may not align with your theology. For that matter, that may be the case with any number of topics covered in this book. A wise mentor of mine once said, "Eat the meat and spit out the bones." If you have made it this far despite some theological disagreements, there is a reason. And that reason is the subject of the final chapter.

If you are interested in learning about land redemption, you can find information about the Wilson's course at:
watchmenarise.com

Chapter 12
An Invitation

"But now I will not treat the remnant of this people as in the former days,' declares the LORD of hosts. 'For there will be peace for the seed: the vine will yield its fruit, the land will yield its produce and the heavens will give their dew; and I will cause the remnant of this people to inherit all these things. It will come about that just as you were a curse among the nations, O house of Judah and house of Israel, so I will save you that you may become a blessing. Do not fear; let your hands be strong.'"
Zechariah 8:11-13

On June 29, 2023, I sat in a quaint little coffee and sandwich shop, preparing to have lunch after spending considerable time in prayer over the final draft of this book. I intentionally sat at the same table I did in January when the Lord met me with a Holy Spirit download that became the initial outline. As I looked around, I was again struck by the simplicity of what God has asked me to convey.

At its core, what was happening in that coffee shop was a representation of the life God intended for humanity. People were building relationships over pleasant conversation while enjoying the blessing of Creation's abundance of food. It really is that simple.

Preparing to say grace over my lunch, I bowed my head and noticed the spread that came with my sandwich. It was made of light oil and—tiny little seeds. As I looked at those seeds, I was filled with an incredible sense of awe. Everything around me—the people with their computers and books, the building, and the plate my food was on—was made possible because of God's incredible design found within Creation, and it all begins with the gift of seed.

After an extended period of saying grace, I enjoyed my lunch. The first eleven chapters of the book were, in some form, in an initial draft. I had yet to title this chapter because I was not sure how He wanted it to end. All I knew was that God asked me to weave together Scripture and present reality in a way that would, by His grace, encourage followers of Jesus to adopt and apply a biblical economic worldview.

Over the next few days, my conversations with God centered around this chapter while I looked at a blank page on my screen. As I continued to press in, God made it clear.

"I want to invite those reading this book to join Me in restoring the covenant I made with humanity in the Garden of Eden."

Reading those words at this moment, I am sobered and humbled at the reality of the majesty of God's Creation and His love for us, codified in a covenant that would ensure we would have the relationships, food, and resources necessary to build His Kingdom.

I am also sobered by the magnitude of the task ahead. God is calling a remnant to embrace this covenant, properly steward Creation, harness the power of trading floors, and consistently deploy micro-deposits that will build and strengthen the body of Christ and our neighbors. Doing so will create a functioning prototype *within His church* of an economic system that has the power to transform communities and nations in ways we can scarcely imagine.

The Holy Spirit directed you to read this book through to the end. How you respond to the invitation is between you and God. Maybe He is asking you to lead a study in your church on the contents of this book. Maybe He is asking you to form a network to begin engaging in trade according to His principles. Perhaps He is asking you to extend that network to include other churches in your community. Or maybe God has given you the resources to buy land and have others steward it to produce food for your community. The point is, He could be asking you to participate in any number of ways. Regardless of what it looks like, God is looking for "a response from His sons and daughters" as we move deeper into this Fourth Turning and the Great Restoration of His principles and ways.

Chapter 12: An Invitation

The Turn Within the Turning

Although it is important to be aware that the kings of the earth are planning a "Great Reset," in reality, as we learned in chapter seven, followers of Jesus have no quarrel with them.[81] Secular leaders have existed throughout history and will be in powerful leadership positions when Jesus returns. While they remain, they will do what they think is best, according to their worldview.

Our responsibility is to steward what God has placed within our jurisdictional authority. For most of us, that will mean strengthening our families and local communities as the shelf-life of the kings-of-the-earth's centralized systems reaches its expiration date.[82] One of the first orders of business is to establish and maintain a functional local economy.

At the time of this revised edition (mid 2025), it is not possible to determine the magnitude and duration of the coming economic and geopolitical disruptions. However, the hope of avoiding major disruptions is beginning to fade as the real battle in the unseen realm intensifies across the earth. Therefore, it is our responsibility to heed the words of Solomon.

> "The prudent sees the evil and hides himself, But the naïve go on, and are punished for it."
> Proverbs 22:3

With that said, let me take a moment and consider the possibility that I am completely wrong about this "fourth turning thing." The world rights itself and a new "golden age" begins. The great thing about this invitation is that you will not waste your time. As I said earlier, God's principles and ways are valid in good times, bad times, and end times. There is still land to be redeemed, food to be made healthy, supply chains to be made resilient, and a biblical economic worldview to be embraced. As you consider taking the first step to join us on this journey, let God's Word encourage you that it is not in vain. In fact, it's quite the opposite. A celebration awaits.

---

[81] Ephesians 6:12
[82] https://www.gostrategic.org/bottom-line-archive/principle-eight-localism-centralization/

"Do not despise these small beginnings, for the Lord rejoices to see the work begin, to see the plumb line in Zerubbabel's hand."
Zechariah 4:10

For those not familiar with this passage, let me provide some context. A plumb line is a simple tool that uses gravity to establish a "true" vertical reference point so that the walls in a construction project do not lean to one side or another. It ensures, among other things, that gravity will hold the walls on the foundation rather than try to pull them over. Perfectly vertical walls are said to be "in plumb," hence the tool's name.

God raised up Zerubbabel to lead the first group of Jews out of Babylonian captivity and back to Jerusalem. He was also commissioned to lead the effort to rebuild the temple—a project that took over twenty years to finish. In this passage, God makes it clear that the first step in a building project initiated by Him is to hang a plumb line—to find the "true" vertical that will help ensure the longevity of what is built. This principle applies whether it is a physical structure, like the temple in Jerusalem, or something more abstract, like an economic system that provides God's people with resources to build a Kingdom.

Hang Your Plumb Lines

One of the primary reasons I wrote *I Came to Give*, *My Ways*, and now *Cultivate and Keep*, is to help followers of Jesus see that the "walls" of the world's economic and monetary systems are badly out of plumb. They were constructed based on a faulty set of principles. Unfortunately, these out-of-plumb "walls" are all that we have known. We have grown so accustomed to them that we accept them as natural and will feel strangely uncomfortable should they change.

This phenomenon is not new. When the Israelites lived in Egyptian bondage for four hundred and thirty years, the "plumb line" that defined Pharoah's economic system—slavery—became normal. When the Israelites were set free, the moment they encountered challenging circumstances they begged to return to the "normalcy"

Chapter 12: An Invitation

of slavery, because it provided them with their basic needs, especially food.

Should the world go through massive cultural, political, and economic changes, you can be certain that many who have accepted the "traditions of men" from the kings of the earth will become quite comfortable with the idea of man's "Great Reset." After all, it will likely seem the quickest way to get "back to Egypt" and a more familiar (and seemingly safe) life. However, rest assured—it is not God's desire that they and their families return to the very real bondage placed upon them by today's economic and monetary systems.

Helping those who attend our local churches to step out of our modern Egyptian economic slavery will not be easy. Some, including your friends and family, may question your sanity as you begin to talk about applying God's principles of cooperation, stewardship, abundance, identity, and sustainability in your community. Others may question the supporting theology. Still others will claim that restoring a covenant with Creation and returning to locally grown food is too "radical" for these modern times. They may in fact, claim it is a step backward in their pursuit of the abundant life Jesus came to give.

In the end, none of that matters to God. His "vertical and true" economic plumb lines are the reference point that the world desperately needs today. Saying "yes" to His invitation puts the plumb line in your hand. It will guide you as you hang it in the literal and figurative "garden" God gives you to tend and you begin to plant seeds in the natural and spiritual realm.

Eventually, those seeds will sprout and grow. As you nurture them, others will take notice and join you. Your collective fruit will become the foundation of a new system of value creation and exchange that is based on a biblical economic worldview. It may take time. However, the day will come when it will be time for another celebration.

> "Now when the builders had laid the foundation of the temple of the LORD, the priests stood in their apparel with trumpets, and the Levites, the sons of Asaph, with cymbals, to praise the LORD according to the directions of King David of Israel. They sang, praising and giving thanks to the LORD, saying, "For He is good, for His lovingkindness is upon Israel forever." And all the

people shouted with a great shout when they praised the LORD because the foundation of the house of the LORD was laid."
Ezra 3:10-11

It is my heartfelt prayer that the Lord will grant followers of Jesus the courage, strength, and wisdom to lay that foundation. Then, should the Lord tarry, future generations can build upon it as humanity enjoys the abundant blessing of honoring His original covenant to cultivate and keep this marvelous Creation and build His Kingdom on earth as it is in heaven.[83]

For more information on how Regeneco can help you respond to God's invitation, visit https://regeneco.org.

---

[83] Matthew 6:10

Acknowledgments

To my wife Kathy. As the journey of our lives has unfolded, I am so thankful that God has seen fit to bring us together in partnership in His work. Having you alongside me as we move into this adventure is a blessing beyond what I can express.

To my children and grandchildren. I am grateful for each day that God gives me the strength to help build a better world for you to live in. Every moment I get to spend with you is precious. I pray that your mom and I get to see each of you walk in the blessing of everything that God restores in the coming years.

Jorge Lorenzana. When God has a plan, He provides the people. My friend, your prophetic voice, embrace of the vision, and your commitment to Regeneco are going to bless the people of Latin America and beyond.

Chris Meidl. The gift God has given me in your friendship and ministry partnership is something I did not see coming. The wisdom and guidance you have brought to me personally and our project is far beyond what you know. And we've just begun.

The Regeneco Team, present and future. Each one of you has the passion and energy to be a world-changer. May the Lord lead us into the future with confidence in our identity as empowered imagers of the one true God.

And once again, to the last, who is the First – my Friend, Brother, King, Lord, and Savior, Jesus. In writing the first three chapters of this book, I grew closer to you than I ever have before. Thank you, my King, for an invitation to work with You to build Your Kingdom.

www.ingramcontent.com/pod-product-compliance
Lightning Source LLC
Chambersburg PA
CBHW071856070526
44583CB00016B/1719